Nathaniel O. V

A MEIN DAN (A BLACK MAN'S) JOURNEY FROM BALTIMORE TO VIET NAM

MEIN DAN
PUBLISHERS

ISBN: 978-0-9799230-8-1

Copyright 2009 by Nathaniel O. Walker, Jr.
All rights reserved. Printed in the United States of America. No part of this book may be used or reproduced in any manner whatsoever without written permission except in the case of brief quotations embodied in critical articles and reviews. For information, address Mein Dan Publishers, 4748 Byron Road. Pikesville, MD. 21208.

DEDICATION

This book is being published in loving memory of Nathaniel Obie Walker, Jr. Obie will be in our hearts forever. He started writing this book over 4 years ago and through many days of various health issues he was able to complete it. It is our intent to carry out his wishes to have this book published.

We'll go down memory lane with Obie as he tells us about his childhood, when he was drafted into the United States Army, and his deployment to Vietnam. His perspective – as a black man – of Vietnam is profound and thought provoking.

His wife Sybil, daughters Shaynee and Shakiera, and son Nathaniel III

TABLE OF CONTENTS

PART I
Chapter 1 - The beginning
Chapter 2 - The hood--lessons of the street
Chapter 3 - Bad day at school!
Chapter 4 - Back to the streets

PART II
Chapter 5 - Uncle Sam calls
Chapter 6 - Basic training
Chapter 7 - To Vietnam
Chapter 8 - Specialized training
Chapter 10 - Trip to the zoo
Chapter 11 - My new home

PART III
Chapter 12 - Getting shot in combat
Chapter 13 - Court martial
Chapter 14 - My son is born
Chapter 15 - Leaving Vietnam

FOREWORD

As I ventured through the lanes to acquire my goal. I saw well-dressed dudes, glittering jewelry, and the charisma of some of the folks that destroy the lives of people without a care. I was a building up a vision of being a "king pin", a self made man of wealth, having no knowledge that it would be on the backs of my own people, destroying thousands and thousands of lives, all in the name of profit.

Now, at the age of sixty I look over my life with amazement of how one at such a young age could have made a decision to start life on the wrong foot. My body, now torn and worn from the abuse I senselessly put myself through, I wrote this book as a message for all young men that have already thought about or actively gone the same path that I started out on.

This is a true story.

PART I

THE BEGINNING

Chapter 1
The Beginning

    This is my story, told the way I want to tell it. I was Born baby boy Walker March 11, 1949 at 1:00 am at the University of Maryland Hospital, Baltimore, Maryland, Westside, to a young couple Delores and Nathaniel Obie Walker, Sr., a very proud father. The couple had lost two children prior to this birth. But they would go on to have 5 more children, 2 boys and 3 girls. Their ages would run like a pair of stair steps, one behind the other. Times would be hard for these two parents and they will separate when I am 8 years old. My mother will then leave me to live with my father and his sister Corrine whom will raise me to manhood. Contact would always remain strong between my mother and myself along with all of the lessons Mom would instill even until this date. And as far as my sisters and my brothers, I become "Little Daddy"; protector, boss and a threat when *Ma* needed help with any of them that got out of line.

    My father remained in the picture telling me what to do in so many situations as for the family and about life's lessons and a far look as what was to come. In fact, my Dad filled my head with plenty of dreams that I aspired to do; and, damn if I didn't do them, not having to say I paid the price for such deeds.

    Well, life with Daddy and Aunt Corrine was very nice. We lived at the top of the hill as it was known, the park was right up the block, shops right around the corner and the top jazz clubs where all the big entertainers came to perform. White people still lived in this area. I had several white playmates. The kids and myself dressed each evening to greet daddy's coming home from work. We even had Peter the Wheatman, and milk delivered right to the door, grapevines, cobble stone backyards, fenced in with a back porch and to boot, the only television on the block along with a telephone. Yes, we were on the hill. Daddy would put the television in the hallway and all of the neighbors would chair up outside on the sidewalk to watch Archie Moore and Joe Louis fight to defend their titles.

This all changed with the separation of Dee (my mother) and Big Obie (my father) and me at 8 years of age. *Ma* moved down the way (as we called it) lower Pennsylvania Avenue part on a little street called Leslie Street across from her old high school "Old" Douglas High School on Calhoun Street and Baker Street. The house was a big old three story, 2 bedrooms with a very small bathroom that would be warm in the summer and freezing during the winter but, the family endured and *Ma* made it work. We called it home even though I didn't stay over many nights, I was always told by *Ma* that this was my home also and never to forget she did not leave me at 18 (2618 Woodbrook Avenue, the house) and always remember she was my mother and never, never would she give me away to anyone, and always respect your father, for us children didn't have a thing to do with the separation.

Well, I missed my sisters and brothers regularly going to *Ma*'s day in and day out, and back to 2618 (18) to tell daddy what was going on. Each time he would get angry and curse *Ma* (that black Hussy) and then go and get a pint of Madiera Dark Port (wine), down it without stopping, get drunk, cuss and damn, then off to sleep. To wake up the next morning, light up a Pall Mall cigarette, smoke, to the bathroom, dress and off to "down the way" and Lord knows what? Then return by 6 p.m. that evening like clock work drunk all over again.

Now, before you judge my father, my old man was a good man, clean, dressed to kill, a ladies' man, gambler, truck driver, long distance tractor trailer driver, husband and father. He had plenty of friends but he had lost my mother; his heart. He also had too many kids in a row and bad times plus a tumor on his brain from a tractor trailer accident that almost killed him and my Uncle Duke. He succumbed to the grapevine and slowly it began to kill him. The drinking and pressures sent him to the crazy house more than 10 times as I count it, to jail several times, nonsupport once and then to blindness. He died at the young age of 44 years old. Poor daddy, he would cry himself to sleep talking about this black hussy (my mother) and how he still loved her. The man never had another woman in his life after their separation. Just wine and loneliness but he had us kids of whom he always bragged about to any one who would listen to his drunk ass.

Yes, at times he made me mad, but he also made me feel so proud during his dry spells. He was meek and taught me a lot of good stuff that still carries me to this day, and most of that stuff I have passed on to my son, Obie, III, oh yea, I love that name. My daddy gave it to me, Big Obie, my Daddy. Now Aunt Corrine who raised me -- short, left handed, yelled a lot, quick to strike, worked like a dog. Man could she cook for Dad and me and all of my buddies and kinfolk. But the most important thing (person) in her life was me. Little Obie, whom never wanted for anything, clothes, food, money, skates, bikes even food.

I would take food to *Ma* and my sisters and brothers. My aunt had to miss all of that tuna, fish, sugar, steaks, lunchmeat, chops, and anything else. I would stuff it into bags to take down the house.

Yes, Rene as I called her was rough, but a real pussycat when you get to really know her and how many times did Rene pull my tired stupid self out of trouble you would not believe. But if Little Obie wanted , all I had to do was to ask Aunt Corrine as I would have all of my boys call my aunt with respect until the day she died and they made the funeral and stood tall for her. But Rene was a *hoss*; tough as nails, quick as lightening, and would hit you with skillets, sticks, shoes, belts or whatever. *Ma*, however was young, alone, resourceful with five kids on welfare. She needed help from anywhere. She was a barmaid, worked in a laundry folding clothes. She cared for my sisters and brothers and played mom and dad as best she could and I must say *Ma* you did a good job. But you paid your dues and some, but I am sure other single moms can understand you and what you had to go through like the good ole times. *Ma* had to do magic with welfare cheese dishes, making her own pork and beans, pan bread, rice pudding, cornbread, biscuits, spam, beef in the can, butter pound cakes, big pots of spaghetti and plenty of beans, apple butter, and grits. We loved it, even when we had to rewrap the toys from the year before. We had a Christmas tree, candy and turkey dinner and all the fixings. Easter was also a big day, new suits, dresses, shoes, the girls had hats and purses.

Ma pushed learning, being on welfare was not going to stop her children from getting ahead, and in time this came to past. To date, oldest girl has a B.S., middle girl, B.S., B.A., M.B.A. and me with a B.S., B.A. in Criminal Justice, Urban Services with a concentration on Urban blight and Effect on population. Middle boy GED, baby boy, now deceased at 43 years old was a U.S. Army Sergeant and held both an A.A. and 100 credits toward a B.A. So the old girl has done well but she still gets on my nerves. Also, *Ma* got off public aid and worked 30 years as a nurses' aide at Baltimore's City Hospital (D&A Buildings Geriatics) and now spends her time at church and trying to run everybody's life. But that's my Mama.

So you now have met some of my people, my home, my humble beginning or gifted beginning and now let's walk on.

Age 13 kicks in and I am now beginning to feel it. I can do my thing. I know the entire neighborhood and parts of all of its surrounding neighborhoods, plenty of people. I now have grown a lot, mostly wide, I wear a 46 trousers and size 16 shirt and 10 ½ shoes. I'm called the "Big nigger ". My clothes are bland because I am so big. Loafers, white shirts, v-neck sweaters, black and white shoes, brogs called (bulldogs) and dessy boots but I have the heart of a jitterbug and I can fight! Nobody, nobody makes fun of me, no one picks on me plus I hang with the big boys, day and night. Anything they do I do. I made this group of young boys my street teachers and teach they did! I experienced a new adventure everyday, all clean fun. But then there was down the way, a difference. Things were tougher, people were different, life was different.

Map of Vietnam

- China
- Myanmar
- Hanoi ★
- Lao PDR
- Ha Tinh
- Hue
- Thailand
- Nha Trang
- Cambodia
- Ho Chi Minh City (Saigon)

Chapter 2
'The Hood'
Lessons from the Street

One day I met my cousin on my mother's side. Cuz was named Dougie. This kid turned out to be my best friend, brother, pal, partner in crime, and partner in the war in Viet Nam. Cuz taught me about Pennsylvania Avenue, the lower part of the City. The flavor of down the way. People of down the way, hustlers, whores, pimps, crooks and the Projects. Cuz was sharp, knew his way around, grown for a young boy, but still a kid.

Cuz introduced me to the Boys Police Club, one of the best things that ever happened to me. At the time Cuz lived across the street from the Club with his big sister Louise, who I adopted as my big sister. Now I had a lot of sisters streetwise that is. But Lou as we called her, was family. Both Cuz and myself owe Lou a lot, God bless her soul. Lou passed a few years back but she will always be with us.

Between home (2618), Leslie Street, Cuz and cousin Louise's house, there was the club on the street and I was learning fast wanting more of everything and all of the experiences I could handle all at once. I was finding ways to make it all come together, at this point I'm street "struck"! School mattered as long as I was there, my mother and sisters and brothers would be taken care of, because I was going to make it so.

I now knew my way around, uptown, and downtown. I was down with certain things. I thought that was where it was at. Slick people, doing slick things, getting things, getting money fast and easy and I wanted it.

During this time there were a few sprinkled, slick, cool cats up on the hill, mostly drinkers. There was jazz and weed for the heads that dug smoke. There was syrup (cough syrup) for those that dug down and pills for those that wanted to float. But then there was *skag*, powder for the ultra cool cats, clean, cool and hustlers they were (super cool). Being young and inexperienced we started serving weed and pills. No way was there any messing with the stuff, just selling it. We had money on the mind, clothes to buy, gold teeth to get, big guy shoes, hats, rings and a roll to flash at will. In short order, we were on our way.

More accepted by the older guys, noticed by the older girls, allowed to go where the older guys went, crap houses, whorehouses, bars, parties, to ride with the hustlers and number writers and enter any and all of the pool halls under age and get to gamble. Most of our clients were full grown men and women at first. We worked outside of the bars, in pool halls and gambling halls. We stayed in certain spots on the strips to sell our wares but we were instructed at all times to stay in school by all of the hustlers. We encountered these men who looked out for us even though they broke the law for a living.

Weird but true, there was a change coming about. More and more people were beginning to drink syrup and pop pills. More people were beginning to dip and nod in plain view, stumble in the streets, not in the shadows or on bar stools or in someone's living room chair. So the pills we sold them, 3 for $1.00 to any and everyone for now the clients were getting younger, even our age. So we supplied them by the mayonnaise jars, carrying them on routes we had set up, to boys or girls, we did not discriminate.

The cleaner we got the better my sister and brothers dressed. Daddy still drank, *Ma* was working, Rene always working and had no idea what I was doing all day long.

Well, summer came and my Aunt sprung on me a job working with her. I had to get a Social Security card and work permit. My father loved this, even said "That's my boy, I am proud of you." I thought, man if you only knew how much money I have stashed on top of the kitchen cabinet.

    This work thing was cramping my style. I was up at 6:30 a.m. catching the bus all the way across town to the white area. I was not use to this, by now most of the whitesshad moved off the top of the hill to the county. Soon and without Cuz knowing it, I was stealing a 'Jay' (reefer joint) every now and again. One day on my break two white boys came out of nowhere as I was smoking in the alley. One asked for a hit and smiled asking if I got any more. Well, off to the races, next thing I knew every day more of his partners were there to meet me on my break. Cuz and I had to buy scales and plenty of bags and tape. Slowly I introduced the pills and was on a roll. There were salt and pepper (white and Blacks) customers, both sides of town. These times seemed like they would never end.

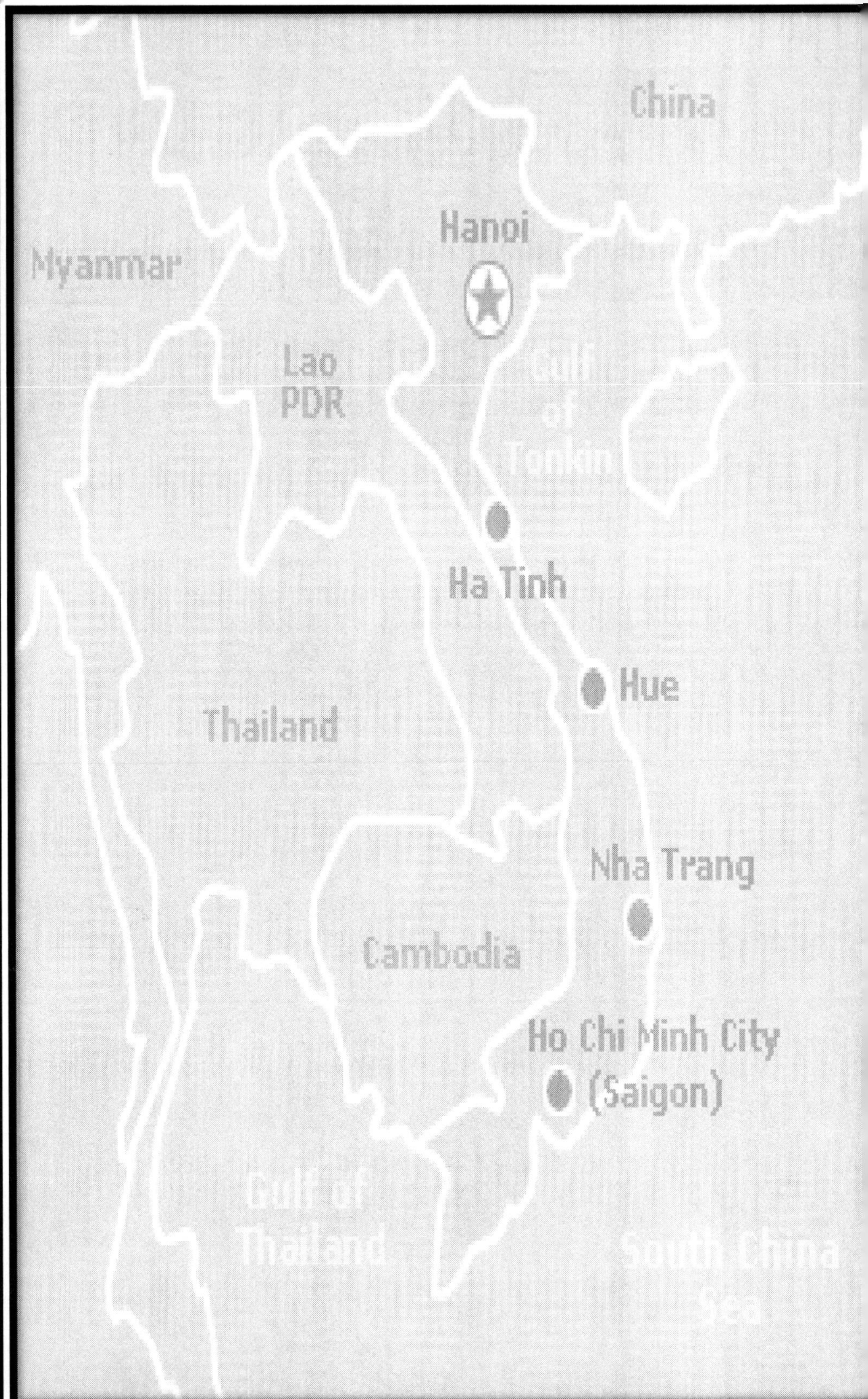
China
Hanoi
Myanmar
Lao
PDR
Gulf
of
Tonkin
Ha Tinh
Hue
Thailand
Nha Trang
Cambodia
Ho Chi Minh City
(Saigon)
Gulf of
Thailand
South China
Sea

Chapter 3
Bad Day At School!

    Well, we made good money every lunch period. I sold some pills to a few dozen girls and they got *twisted* and I was told on for selling the pills. The police were called into the school. My locker was popped open. I didn't even know the cops were looking for me in the school building. I was in between classes selling pills in the bathroom when I found out the girl told on me. I left the school, went to the mall across the street from the school to hide.

    While trying to hide, three guys I knew approached me, bought nine pills from me, and went on. I had no idea these guys intended on robbing the bank facing the school. They knocked (robbed) the bank tellers off by jumping the counters. The police filled the Mall. I ran out of the Mall straight into the school where a shop teacher saw me, confronted me about being out of class at the wrong time. They caught me just as the police who were looking for a kid with a red Parka, Vienna shirt, and black pants with gator (alligator) shoes on and that was me.

    They charged me with the pills, money, and selling drugs on school grounds. This all happened two weeks before graduating from the 12th grade but I was still a juvenile so I missed jail and only got kicked out of school. The school took my picture out of the yearbook, no sheepskin for me. I was an embarrassment to my family and myself. My teachers could not believe it, not Nathaniel, no not him: Yeah! Him.

    So now I really belong to the streets, I am lost and do not know what to do with myself. I thought I might be granted a break, my mother was praying for one. Together we went to the School Board pleading for re-entry to school. This fell on deaf ears, I was blackballed from all city schools.

Still trying, we found out that a county school might be more forgiving. Well, God heard our prayers. The school was 33 miles away so if I was serious about education I had to get up at 6 am to travel down on the number 7 bus line, get off at the Civic Center, then try to hitch a ride with anyone going towards Washington, DC.

To all those kind people that picked this young Negro up, thank you very much with all my heart. Thank You! I went each day even on the days the school was closed or delayed because of snow, I rode with someone trying to get there. Now I had lunches, brown bag type, supplied by Aunt Corrine from her job, ham and cheese, turkey with Swiss cheese, tuna with the works, name it, I had it plus pies and cakes to boot. I also had $2.00 of which $.50 for bus fare, $.25 each way to downtown. I attended school faithfully, did well for the most part, but I still had my little hustle going on, a dream to complete.

Chapter 4
Back to the Streets

I still sold pills and weed each night upon getting back home. I also had received my draft papers from the U.S. Army with draft number 900 or so but it was in the 900-1000 for sure. My cousin had also got his draft call and number just after completion of the 12th grade. We both knew we might get assignments to go to Nam.

Neither of us knew much about this place or what was going on there but were found out there was a long ongoing war over in Indochina, where? Well, whatever, we knew we would not be called to serve anyway. By now Cuz had stumbled upon another source to get us paid. This new product was suppose to be a real winner and in high demand. We went down on Pennsylvania Avenue. We ended up in the back of a hairdresser's shop. There we met our new boss. I was shocked to find out the man that was giving us the pills was now to give us the "Junk". Decisions, decisions, this was a big step, but money is money. I still had my job at the restaurant, had a raise of $2.50 more, now $200.00 a week and all I could steal, for I worked the dining hall as a kitchen porter and cut rate assistant. I retrieved beer from the ice boxes and liquor from the shelves as a stock boy. I loved it, each day I would stash pints and fifths in the trash can, I enriched my pay check

But now we are beginning to work in the big times. We need something more, a ride (car). Well, a summer back I worked at a car dealership. I had waxed, buffed out new cars for the showroom and jockey the cars from hold lots to dealerships without a driver's license. I had lied about my age to obtain the job. I blew it playing around on the ramp with one of the brand new rides as I tore up two other cars by hitting gas instead of the brakes. But at least I kept my weed (marijuana) customers as I got escorted off the property. Well, I always had a thing for GTOs (Goat) speed on top of style. Well, one night after working at the cut-rate and selling my "Old Grand Dad" 80 and 100 proof, Carstairs, 4 Roses, Gordon's Gin, I shared a pint of Old Crow, got drunk as a skunk. I stole a 1963 Chevy Impala. These cars had easy ignition switches, so it was not a great feat to steal it. Well, Cuz and I drove around the neighborhood until I ran out of gas and left the car parked safely a block from where I stole it.

Well, we caught a jones (habit)-a car jones. There weren't many cars around the block, so we sought out the college up on the hill where all of the whites went to school, plenty of vehicles were there for the picking. So we started collecting cars. We, Cuz and myself, knew all of the empty buildings in our area. When we walked the area, we decided to use this garage that was a huge warehouse that had stood empty for a couple of years. We checked the back and found a way in by scaling the wall, found our way to the bottom floor. We found the two huge entrance doors, just what we hoped for. We stole cars, upon cars, GTO for me a Lemans for Cuz. Every Sunday we would cruise in our hot cars. Cuz couldn't drive so I was out to teach him how. We stole a 1963 Chevy and went to the park. Cuz took the wheel, jerking, stopping, driving a few feet, stopping on the road and the grass until he found the road. The blacktop, 10 mph, 20 mph, 30 mph, turning, backing up, the radio on, testing the wipers, man he was doing it. We did this again and again, now all along life was going on. Cuz was still doing the school thing. I was now working and stealing at the restaurant, selling lunchtime weed and junk to the white boys, then home to my post on the Avenue awaiting Cuz to join me. Our post was right between a bar and restaurant with a little cubby space next to a phone booth with a good view of everything going on in the block plus the intersecting streets to the north and south and west of our post. The No. 9 bus lines, six bars and two cut rates and later one pool room. Things were going well, business was good. Now, on the hill most of our customers were working men. They partied on the weekend mostly. Then there were a few that copped a bag of weed in the middle of the week but not many. So, while Cuz was in school, I hung around anywhere on Wednesdays, my day off from the restaurant roaming around, but mostly down the bottom of Pennsylvania Avenue.

While everything else was going on, a new drug wave was at its peak. These scenes I never experienced on top of the hill. There were hundreds of people walking, running around all with one thing in mind, buying dope. There were people waiting in alleys, on corners, dealers selling junk out of their cars. Women were acting as in between dealers, men with guns in the open. This was like a cowboy picture, the wild west. Pills could be bought, weed, syrup, junk. This was an open market. No police anywhere. Wow! All of these people were clean, dressed well, cool cats and chicks. Even the whores looked good. And all of this was going on right on the same block where a brand new drug center had just open.

Yes, a drug center, fresh from New York City. Baltimore had introduced drug treatment called "Biscuit". This stuff had been introduced in NYC and was said to help calm the craving for Boy, Horse, Gee, Skag, Her-Run-Her-Run. Project Adapt, the sign stated. You couldn't tell the place was even there, that's how I saw it to be. But my street knowledge was just starting, for now I was seeing the other side of drugs, real users, hustlers, players, and crooks. But I needed a guide, and Cuz was right there, growing up down the way, exposed to things I had only heard about Cuz was down with. Ready as I thought I might had been, my mother had other plans. *Ma* had the wheels rolling straight towards me getting back in school. Even if I wound up being 21 finishing high school.

Well, once again to 23rd Street in Baltimore City to the School Board we went, pleaded for my re-entry to finish my education. I offered no resistance. I wanted back badly because I liked school, plus everyone I knew was in school. I was all worked up about it…"But there was a catch, yes I would have to go to an alternative school, not my old high school." Well, I had messed up. I was lucky they let me back, plus I could still obtain that piece of paper, a high school diploma. That was ok with me. I started my new journey that following week, starting like all of the other students, but miles away from where I had once been, a new start, new people and surprisingly I liked the school. I was doing well and with my new found hustle, I had a few coins. I was really in charge at lunch time. I could buy two and three chocolate milks, buns, cake and a lunch plate. I mingled at all of the hip tables and had the girls wondering who I was, plus I was clean and halfway slick, but I had plans, get the diploma, get a half-ass good job, save some money, buy some dope (weight) make money and be the man.

Report cards showed I had potential and a couple of instructors pulled me up and questioned me, how I ended up there. Being cocky but honest, I told them all I didn't plan on working all my life and had plans on being retired and having everything I wanted by the age of 45 years old. All of the adults just smiled with a worried look upon their faces. Time marched on, my studies were hitting the mark. The environment was what I needed. This adult learning school was ok. While cruising the halls one day a bulletin board caught my eye, a new program was starting up called GED, that excelled ones getting their papers fast after taking a few major classes, English, Math, Science, History and Literature and passing to obtain a raw score of 1500 points. Well, I knew I could do this and I went right at this program. Man, not only did I work this program and passed it, I found a new hustle. I started testing for anybody and everybody (males). I spread the news around. Money was coming in faster than I could get phony ID cards made up for all of the men I tested for. The men at the testing class got wind of me in short order. So, they were put on payroll. I was scared to death of the women testers. They would tell on me and everybody else, I just knew it, so I slid in and out of the four testing classes every two weeks. The tests were given four hours per test. Most test days I did two tests a day starting at 7:30 a.m. I got damn near all of my home boys and my brother Noddie a GED. He is retired now, things were fine, but there was a lot of work being put out on my part, all along my mind was on getting more money, being the man. Well, I was testing so much, I had to be noticed, and I was, this supervisor confronted me, asking me all types of questions with her eyes dead on my name badge. The woman made sure she pulled me up in front of the testing agents and kept on coming back with questions. Well, the testers got together and hit me up. They would have to cut me off. I was angry, but what could I do, with knowledge of them having their own ringers taking tests for them and all of us were getting paid, but now I was out of the game. But I had a back up that I could work full time, plus I still had my job at Aunt Corrine's job as a busboy/porter for Social Security earnings for retirement and a way to hide the unlawful funds I planned on making before I turned 45 years old. Well, regroup time.

Back to Woodbrook/Pennsylvania Avenue, the world, money! Now with this regroup, I must regress! We have walked a while together, but if there is a beginning and we'll get to the end, there must be a middle. So off we go. No more easy money. No more GED testing. I blew that ok. So I go back to full time to what I know or should I say what I am learning the hard way. Well, whatever, I have plenty of home boys and most of them were still there when I left them in the neighborhood and surrounding neighborhood even ready to see me come home. Because shop would open as soon as I hit the door, drugs for sale. My poor Aunt Corrine would leave at 6:30 a.m. each day, off on Wednesdays only, her out to work, me to the alleys, waiting in their cars around the corner, all around. I was popping, Cuz would come pass on his way to school, bring up more product to be handled until he got home. We had herb and skag and pills. Things had come together for us, the man, our customers, all was well.

Then one day the phone company truck came into the block, they set up and it seemed they had come to stay. White boys all over the place. Now, I knew every house on the block and who had what and there was only five phones in the 2600 block for sure so what in the hell were these people doing setting up camp around here and worst than that, there wasn't any work going on at all, but I worked on day after day, watching. Plenty of days the phone company workers sat and watched the going and coming of our clients. Time after time I would walk over to the hole they had dug in the street and sidewalks to look at the work they were suppose to be doing. One of the supposedly foremen had even started to talk to some of the neighborhood women and kept sending the kids to the corner store during their breaks and lunch times. Yea, they were really trying to blend in now. Now I have a best friend, brother, pal, stickman named June Bug. A few years younger than myself, but he was my main man. We stuck together for years but June Bug couldn't stand Cuz and Cuz knew we were cousins, and blood was thick, plus June Bug's's girl thought Cuz was the shit. So I just watched them go back and forth, but I kept the peace.

Now, June Bug was my walking buddy, friend, partner in crime, peace, war, no doubt he would go down with and for me. And I got along better with Cuz and June

Bug than I did with my own brothers. Mostly cause *Ma* had stated she didn't want us brothers to hang together. One get in trouble, both of her sons would end up in trouble, so stay apart, you might be the one to save your brother's life one day by people not knowing you are brothers. There was no worry about our younger brother because *Ma* has little Larry safely kept (home). Well, me and my stickman June Bug went in and out of a lot of adventures; mostly, when I was in the process of re-upping of the drugs we had sold out. Money, more money on the mind, crap games, cards. Still too young to get into the poolrooms even though Cuz could get into the poolrooms. Some of the old men dug his style and carried him in with them and the kid could shoot, no doubt! But June Bug was the sole master of a pair of dice. The boy had long slender fingers, with the slickest shake man has ever seen, followed with this funny flick of his wrist, the dice would hit the concrete and point. We would pick up! Oh yea! Man those old dogs would cuss like hell had just broke open.

My man would stay squatted like a China man shaking the dice he had just picked back, stating ready to see the young man go again. Now plenty of times things got hot, hot to trot. But we couldn't show any fear at the beefing. We never would be able to come back, plus we would lose face, also get robbed and our butts kicked! Young, but not dumb! We had our knives and an old .22 caliber revolver pistol but the barrel would fall out but we had a gun. It was hidden on top of Aunt Corrine's kitchen cabinet along with our stash, unknown to anyone but me and my dog Blackie (that's between me and you).

Our gambling took us around schoolyards, recreation centers, ball diamonds, tracks, basketball courts, school dances, roller-skating rinks, then back to the corner crap games, anywhere. They hated but loved to see us come for we had money, possible money they could win. But the worst games were right in the neighborhood. The older guys would gamble every Friday - Sunday evening with some day games. Knowing one another and one another's weaknesses and strengths too much shit would be in the game, getting broke, begging, taking turns cutting on an outside game, taking money back from the weaker guy if he just happen to win from a stronger guy. You really had to stand your ground. Well, just so happen the brick was to hit the wall. June Bug had the dice, sitting like a China man kicking butt! Then up comes one of the local number writers. Well known to all owner of houses, money lender to the welfare mothers, lending $.25 on a dollar, a cold trick to plenty of the housewives, a player. Well, he jumps in the game after lending out a few hundred dollars to the side losers, he starts to try to break up the winning streak June Bug and I have going on with each roll of the dice he would bet $10.00, $20.00 , $40.00, $50.00, betting money like there is no end to his knot. He was getting into the hustle money but (F) him. We are going to hang. "You don't", was all he said, over, over, over and over again and again. Now all of those that were hanging on were in the mix. I had to whisper to June Bug (Man) he looked over at me, almost angry and shook the dice, shook his head. At least 4 minutes passed. This one guy, a semi pro football player who everybody was ¾ scared of was hassling us with every shake of the dice was wide open talking straight (Sh-) "Yea, you little son of a black bear, you motherless son of a dog, you this, you that! What you gonna do now, you greasy monkey!! You and that extra black bastard (that's me) what you gonna do." Well, shake, shake a flick of the wrist, a pair of duces, yes 2+2 little Joe! Oh yea! Ground Hog! The ground looked like a bushel of collar greens, still sitting like a China man June Bug was picking up cash. I had picked up piles of money, money still on the ground. That nigger said something like (F) that or whatever and sprung into action grabbing cash, my boy tried blocking him, grabbing cash up under himself and trying to fight this fool off. It was turning into a free for all. All of the wall hangers and onlookers were now in the mix! Well, to hell with the money, that nigger was trying to kick my boy's guts out of his back. I hit my pocket, hit my hook-bilt knife, gonna kill this bitch, and I stepped forward. Gonna judge this fool, thrust forward and is stopped, choked in the death lock, and told Spade it ain't worth it. The choker is one of the guys that all of these locals not only respected but admired, he did not work. Had just come home from the Joint but was known at the major crap games and would fight anyone. But as he held me choking the shit out of me, he had pushed that fool off of my boy who was standing on the main bulk of money left on the ground. His presence has quieted down a lot of the action. Out of no where, this sneaky, low-life, piece of dog mess crept up to the side of him and slapped; yes, slapped the taste out of my mouth. This sneaky dog had fingernails that cut my face and had the nerve to step away talking stuff. With all that going on, the number writer was standing outside all of the mess shaking his head and said that was good for a youngster, then walked on.

 I was released, thank God! Catching my breath I didn't say a word. We scoped the crowd to see who we were going to get back, drunk or sober, blind, cripple or crazy, their asses was out. They had robbed us, now we had a riff going on for sure, plus we were going to tell our homeboys what had come off. The old heads had jumped us youngsters and we were going to tell our man we had been taken off for his money for sure. And I was going to get that snake who slapped me and get that fool for trying to kill my boy. We would get them. Now we had neighborhood cops who had allowed the crap games with no hassle at all. The games were mostly always non-violent, no problems at all but this had caused a lot of talk and people were watching now for the youngsters to strike back.

No sooner than the following Friday the supposedly phone repairmen were on the poles stringing all kinds of lines. Our party line phone had all kinds of clicking sounds on the line. The white people talking in the background, all kinds of wild stuff, different groups of phone repairmen day and night workers. The beat cop was walking the alley, standing on the corner, business was slacking off. People were walking pass but no stopping to cop, so I took on a couple of homeboys to walk the edges of the block, hit the clients on the move. I had a four block square covered for sales. It was working swell, but it was being watched and noted. We knew by all means we were on the map because people were coming from way outside of our area, a lot of strangers, friends of friends buying pick ups for their friends and stuff.

Things were so good I even had my first stick-up man come to take me off. During those days, we could work out of our pockets. It was nothing to have 125 bags of stuff in one's pocket, 25 bags a bundle or 12 bags a ½ a bundle at $3.00 a bag was nothing new or unusual. Well, I was serving clients in my back alley by this time I saw faces known to me. We had run together in the street, went to school together, gone to dances, games, recreation clubs together, then to have a homey pull a gun on me! He told me to kick the dope and cash in. Now, I was blown away! My man was sticking me up. All of the things we had gone through, times we had shared, damn! We had hustled together, stole yo-yos from the $.05 and $.10 stores together, ran ball together and now he had thrown down on me for some junk, with a gun, ready to take me off! Was this real, well shit here we stand! Now, I know he's no killer, but has a gun, small but a gun, he is not shaking, sweating, but will this so and so kill me? But if he takes this dope I'm through. Word will get out and every stick up man in town will be coming at me. On top of that, my man will throw me away for being so weak. Well, how do

I show, but I have a lot of joints in my pockets and a stash of cash. Man, I'm fucked.

    I don't really know where the rap came from but my mouth started to run within seconds I took that nigger back to the playground, walking my dogs, chasing our home girls, hooking school, me covering his ass when he was banked by some of our enemies of old. I hit the head! Man you don't want to really do this! All you had to do was tell me you were doing bad! You know, we go man! Why this, huh? Why this? The reply was "Man I don't want to hurt you Blackie, just kick the shit in." This was more a plea than a demand or that's how I heard it. I reached into my pocket, pulled out a small one, ½ a bundle, 6 bags of shit, stating here is two for your jumper, 2 for later and 2 for later tonight. Come over tomorrow morning by 7:30 a.m. and you start to work with me, alright? Silence from both of us. The gun was lowered, my man reached out took the package, nodded, both of us turned our heads to the left, there had been a small group of buyers looking on that neither he nor myself had even thought about with their wide-eyed selves waiting to see what was going to come off.

    Since homey had the piece, I played it up! If you mutha fuckas want to cop, come on. Homey stood by my side and we served those clients and then we strolled towards my backyard, up the back stairs, in the kitchen, sat down, shot some drugs of which I supplied free of charge, and got high. I found out my boy's man had put him and the rest of his crew down with their re-up drugs so I suggested, send your clients this way and you make a buck a bag which was my cut of sales I made for the short run than when you get re-upped again. We can hook up as partners and never worry about down time again and keep our people happy, the combine re-ups with constant supply of stuff and quality that will stay tight, we can mix our packages together to assure the shit is good so we won't fuck one another. Well, it sound good! This could work! The more we talked, the more we agreed to do just that! Then my boy confessed that he was put up to the stick up by some of our other boys, yea homeboys that were suppose to be alright with me! He had left them on hold awaiting him to come back and share the bounty with them. This information blew my mind, but taught me not to trust so-called homeboys, friends from then until now, where dope or money was concerned, but it taught me to be fair with someone who was down and out.

Well, we did team up, made some cash, but grew apart because time and situations and the love of the drugs changed the both of us. Also, he took to sticking up again and got killed trying to stick up a bar in 1971, a shame, I liked that boy, I really did. I did play the funeral and sign this book for his people, rest in peace.

But as I was saying the neighborhood was on fire because of the shit that had come off at the crap game. June Bug had his ass stomped, I was choked; that nigger slapped me, my knife is back in my pocket, and we are going to get them back. Cops are hot on our tails, phones are tapped we think, phony phone company, people are suppose to be working all shifts. Well, it's just another day on the job, I am sitting out back on the porch, a nice day. Now sitting out there all day, day after day can be boring so I needed something to do. There was a new kind of haircut that was catching on. The Crovatis, it was round shaped in the front, shaped side burns, squared or rounded in the back, sharp, no lie. Rags or a jar of grease needed to slick your mop. Well, well! All one needed was some sharp clippers, blades, a sheet, a chair and a steady hand and a little skill which could be learned at the barber school (Apex) right on the Avenue. In a few months I knew I could do anything or so I believed, so I bought a pair of clippers and blades, even got after cut good smelling Tonic.

I had a kitchen chair, had sheets in the house, kept a big safety pin handy somewhere. I opened a mini backyard barbershop. Well, thinking once again this would cover up all of the traffic that was coming and going, something to keep me from being bored, plus it would confuse the hell out of the phone company people and the police trying to watch everything and everybody. Man, I was on! Every little nappy-headed boy for blocks around was coming to the house. Then the big sisters were bringing their little brothers, Moms bringing their sons telling me how they wanted it cut this short and put a part that long, square that, round this. They taught me how to cut hair and I listened to them word for word, stroke for stroke, cause I was not about to refund any those $.50 a cut (shit) burning my Aunt's electricity, plus I had to buy dog food for my dog. Now, since I had the shop going on my crew could hang, people could come and go in and out the alleys. Some of the clients even got cuts, especially the young girls. They would come get their "kitchens" cleaned up (shaped) and flirt with me. My Aunt was alright with it. I was working, honest work. The poor woman knew no wrong to be done by her nephew. She liked all the kids calling her Aunt Corrine, all of my homeboys calling her Aunt Corrine, even carrying her bag from the bus stop.

Everybody loved Aunt Corrine and on her day off from work she would feed my customers, fixing pots of meatballs and spaghetti, grilled cheese sandwiches, soup or beans with ham hocks and cornbread. Some people, young and old only came to get cuts on Wednesdays to eat (for sure) and she loved every minute of it. But dum-t-dum dum! Did I mention, Aunt Corrine's house was two doors from a real barber shop. Well, it was, well I was short stopping his business and the shit hit the fan. Between that shop and a couple of more barber shop owners of which I respected and still do today, couldn't tolerate me and the loss of all of those nappy heads complained and complained. Until I was on the back porch cutting, four or five customers waiting, sitting on the porch steps, a big sister and mother sitting on my homemade bench on the porch, radio playing, some corn (white shoe peg) butter in the butter dish, not margarine now! My boys in the backyard playing spades, drinking kool-aid on the rocks with a sun-brella, dog under the table sleeping, a bomb goes off. Boom!

Yelling, police running into the alley, both ends of the alley and a new thing a police German shepherd dog. Man! I could not believe this! All of these police, men in suits, the dog barking, the customers upset, my boys freaked out of their minds. I'm shook, those fools have knocked my Aunt's front door down, they are in the house, they are trying to start a search. I've got to stop this! I fake off, loud as hell, pushing past this bunch of invaders into the kitchen. I took them off guard! What the hell are ya'll doing in my house. Hey, you white boy, don't touch that, what the fuck is wrong with you! I did not hear the dog barking, I did not care about their guns, I did not care about their badges, all of those blue uniforms they didn't mean a hill of beans. They were about to tear Aunt Corrine's house up! Every eye was on me, huffing and puffing, I was ready to take them all on. When a voice, a voice from in our hallway said, "Wait a minute!"

This big black man in a gray suit, no hair on his face, parked the blue uniforms to the front of the group, it was motionless, quiet as a mouse, the man 6 feet and a few inches, 260 pounds or better, nice shoes and tie, then spoke slow and calm and said, "Son you are breaking the law. "You are in violation of operating a commercial barber shop in a residential unit, possible permit violation creating a public nuisance and running a nuisance house and I must state possible drug dealing, distribution, sales and possession, do you understand these possible charges son? This gives us reason for the situation you now find yourself in." I stood there, then I said, "Well you are wrong about the drug stuff, ain't no drugs in this house Mister so ain't no reason for kicking my Aunt's door down and all of these people acting all crazy about to tear my Aunt's house up." The big man said, "Is that right," touched his chin, smiled, looked around at his boys, looked back at me saying, "I'll bet you are right about that. Well, you wouldn't mind if we look around huh?" "You can look all you want, ain't no drugs in my Aunt's house, Sir."

The big black police turned away, said something to this white cop Sergeant with stripes on his sleeves, then back to me. "Ok, we will see." Now I peeped past the uniforms down the hall towards the door opening, the door was hanging on one hinge, the street had police cars, plain cars and the block was full of on-lookers, all of my Aunt's neighbors, oh man and it's 2:30 p.m.

Aunt Corrine will be in at 5:00 p.m. sharp, oh God! My eye was back on the big black cop and his boys. Then I scoped all of these light blue shirts, those damn phone company suppose to be workers, yea, I was right, phone company my ass! The foreman with my boys grouped up like sardines in a can. Yea, a phone company alright. The Sergeant took the two women past us standing between the kitchen and the dining room down the hallway to the living room. Five cops with hands on passed us the same way towards the front doorway where my Aunt's broken front door hung on one hinge to the police cars. I don't know when they let the little kid go or what happened to my clippers and blades and sheet.

My dog was relocated to the pound, he didn't like police anyway, probably acted the fool. The majority of the group thinned out to the front and hanging around their cars, big black Sergeant, me and at least 6 police detectives was still standing tall. Big black said "Search!" I said "But don't tear my Aunt's house up please." Sergeant said "Sit down." I sat down in the chair next to the kitchen window overlooking the backyard. Three cops still out there, looking all around the ground. In the dog house in the next yard, trash cans, fools I thought. Big black sat watching me as I tried to watch everything his boys was doing. They were good, they looked in, around, under, over everything, the oven, the fridge, cereal boxes, ice cub trays, heat vents, towel drawer, china closet, sugar dish, colanders, cookie jar, down the cellar. I heard, then saw the two women walk out the front door. I heard, then saw, Sarge talking to some of the cops, door slamming closed, the engines start, then they drove off.

As I look down the hallway, the people were leaving the crowd thinning out. The door still hanging on that damn hinge, cellar done, the cops coming upstairs, shook their heads, then up the stairs to the second floor. shit ! They are going to go into Aunt Corrine's room, damn it, damn! Big black saw the dread in my face as I sighed, "See what you have brought to this woman's house." He said, "Yea" I said, "Man!" black hollered over his right shoulder, "Hey careful in the old lady's room now. Leave it as you found it! I mean this, you hear me." "Yes Sir!" someone replied then he turned to me. We just looked at one another not saying a word. But he felt the *thank you Sir*.

I look over at the toaster and wall behind it that held the clock, 3:55 p.m., time slipping away. Black was watching me, said "Soon she'll be home huh? Can I have something to drink, please." I got up, got a clean glass rinsed it, to the fridge, got the ice cube tray, Sarge came back so another glass I got, rinsed it, ice in the glasses, back to the fridge reached two 16 oz Lotta cola's, popped the caps and set them before the both of them. None for you son. Now, plenty of movement above our heads, doors shutting, dragging around the floors. Those cops were putting the search on, but I sat there awaiting for them to hit the shit. Because they were getting into my father's room. Then damn, damn! Came from up there (Sarge) stood up all excited! Up the stairs he flew, black looked at me smiling. He said "Let's go," up we went. These cops were standing around like a bunch of little boys. Daddy had all kinds of mortar shells, dummy head grenades, knives, razors with pearl handles, hookbilts, spoon knives, Army helmets, gun caps, overcoat, pea coats, sea rations, ribbons and pickle jars of jump steady homemade wine in my clothes cupboard. Big black said "A bootlegger huh?" "Well, we aren't looking for that". Someone said, "Well that's all there is Sir." Big black said, "There ain't no drugs in his Aunt's house. Well, I guess you're right huh?" "Yes, I said." "Well, you'll still going to jail son." I said ok, but not for no drugs as I look at my favorite phone company worker. "But what about the front door huh?" Big black smiled, Sarge spoke, "The city will fix it." You have to submit a claim. "A claim that ain't gonna happen today, right?" No answer from either of them.

    Sarge went to his hip cuffs, clicked open. I looked out the front door way there across the street in front of the plumbing company Gordon and Sollers was one of my homeboys. I hollered out to him, got his attention called out to him, go around to Mr. Johnson's house. Mr. Johnson was the steelworker with a side line job as all around handyman. This man was known to fix anything and I sure needed him to hook that door back up ASAP. My boy took off towards the direction of Mr. Johnson's house which was around the corner down the block a little bit. Man I felt relieved the door would be in place before my aunt got home.

    To Western District I was going for sure. Since we, meaning me and my boys were juveniles, no police paddy-wagon was called. We were driven in police cars to the station, a social worker interviewed us all. One at a time and alone from one another but all of the stories came out the same. We weren't doing anything and surely didn't know anything about selling any drugs. The only worry we had was our parents would be called into the mix. Now that was something to think about. Now the big black man and Sarge were not on the scene. I almost missed their presence cause they were cool.

Sitting in the station in separate cells in the back of the jail wasn't too cool. We joked and laughed about who was coming to the real big jail down in Jessup where the real jail birds were. It was getting late, we knew because the cops were loud outside of the holding area, we would hear the changing of shift workers plus some of them back to look at us like we were in the zoo or somewhere. This I hated knowing they were making mental records of us all even if my boys never thought of this factor.

They gave us sandwiches and coffee for dinner and finally some toilet paper, then the guard came back to open the cells. We lined up, marched outside to a truck down somewhere to juvenile hall holding, processed again, then led to a big sleeping and recreation area hall. It seemed that hours passed. One by one my homeboys were called, they left the area not to come back homebound. I was thinking, hours passed, then a few more, well lights out. I'm the only one left, my mother nor Aunt Corrine or my father had shown. I just knew my shit was out. They were not with me! Morning came and so did some food, egg sandwiches and milk. Then more waiting, then Walker, Jr.. alright! I slow walked down this hallway to this room. There first off was Big black, my Aunt and father, this lady and a empty chair. I sat down. I was told I was being charged with a nuisance house charge. I waited for the other shoe to fall and heard nothing else. I was puzzled as I looked at everybody in the room. The lady said this charge was going to be enforced in a matter of a stet, what? That was governed by rules that if I violated this order not to be involved in the same kind of activity again in one year I could be charged and sent away for a period of no less than two years in a correctional institution.

    I was glad but I knew not to crack a smile because no one else was smiling. All the way home in the taxi, it was super quiet. We reached the house, I just wanted to get there to see the door and to get upstairs to see what the cops had messed up. The door didn't look any the worse for being knocked off its hinges, downstairs was straight as I had last seen it but upstairs I wondered. Not a word was said, yet by my parents nothing, nothing at all! I jumped up the stairs, eyes wide open, man! My room was cleaner than I had left it, the bathroom looked good, I peeped into my father's room, straight, whew! I breathed, now Aunt Corrine's door was shut, wasn't going in there, back down the stairs I went. I walked into the kitchen, sat down in the same chair I had set for big black. My aunt at the sink, my father sitting at the head of the table just sitting there. I looked out the window for Blackie my dog. Daddy said "We will go get him from the pound later today boy". Then he got up. Daddy was sober, he never said much when he was sober. I knew he was upset, worried even. This affected me, daddy disappeared into the living room sober man sober. Still not a word from my aunt.

    Finally, my aunt spoke, "Dope, the man said you been selling dope out of my house boy!" Her octave getting louder and louder, the dishwater was jumping now. I didn't see any dirty dishes when I had sat down in that chair. She was building up too a fever I knew it, like I remember this crazy woman using skillets, brooms, pots anything to express her anger. So, I had my eyes on her, "You didn't have no dope in my house I know, did you?" I still hadn't said a word. Just as she tried to ask me again a knock at the door, whew! Daddy answered it. Mr. Johnson come to get paid for the lock and hinges for the door. Just enough time to have things cool off. I eased off into the living room with my dad. He sat at the window looking out, the television was on.

    I heard Aunt Corrine going up the stairs, her bedroom door open. Whew! No screaming, her room and things must be alright. I was thinking, my thoughts were interrupted by my father, his voice low, slowly he said, "Boy why are those boys of yours crawling all around that cigar tree out back in Mrs. Shirley's yard, huh? And what's in them penny bags? You know anything about that Obie? Do you?" I just sat there, not a sound, not a word! We sat, we watched television until we were called to eat dinner. My father never told my aunt about the tree, that I know of and I knew my father knew. What a piece of shit I was. But I was his son and he loved me. Now me and my boys were considered heroes by the dumb young people.

    We had beat the cops and we, especially me, a damn fool and a little hoodlum by the adults. Someone to be watched, plus I had betrayed my aunt and had the police at the poor woman's house as they saw it. I was worthless, shameful. But I was mad at the barbers for blowing a tip and sending the man at me. So, I decided to set up shop away from the house. But not too far from the house, just one alley away from the house. Just one alley away from the original alley and our yard and the back porch and house plus I still would have a four way in and out of the alleys for my clients and now a new attitude about the police, phone workers and anybody else strange to the neighborhood. I still had to get money regardless, that's right I didn't sleep much, trying to think how to regroup, wondering where Cuz was, did he know what had come off. Should I tell our man the police had found our stash and the cash we had made, so many things to think about, what to do.

    Morning came. Daddy up by 6:00 a.m., he kicked my bed, feet on the floor was his get the hell up boy, wake up boy, signal up. I got washed up, down the stairs. I went, awaiting me in the kitchen, he was. Got to get going was all that was said. Now, I didn't know where to go to get the dog back so I am ready. We started to walk towards down the way. As we walked, people started to speak to my father, men he has known. Not saying a word to me, we walked on, we were almost downtown, big downtown Baltimore. I don't know hardly anything about this part of town, so I'm keen to pay attention to everything. The building, big cars all over the place and wall to wall white people. Man, this place is jumping with activity. We snaked through alleys, up long blocks, down narrow streets. I'm looking at all of the street signs trying to remember their names for I know my father will dodge me and leave me to find my own way back home, just to see if I was paying attention to where I was going.

So, I'm on watch. We get near the Harbor, I know parts of the Harbor because I had been here with my father and his buddies when they hustled trucks working fruits and veggies unloading. I feel like I'm on solid ground now. The shock of twists and turns are all but gone away. We clear the Harbor front onto where houses started up again. Daddy spoke about a lot of stevedores and longshoremen live down here. "You can get your butt beat real easily down here son." I listened and looked about. Daddy never talked like that because I had heard how good he was with a knife and a razor so I respected this information finally.

We reached an industry area where the dog pound was. We entered, gave the papers up and the five dollars to get our dog back. The woman took our papers, then a man came forth, he looked kind of funny, stated that Blackie was gone! Gone, what? I mean he is dead, "What the hell are you talking about?" my father said with a grumble in his voice, "Dead?" We put him to sleep, "Sleep what?" Now, this man in a dog catcher's uniform came out of a room to the right of us asking if everything was alright.

"Hell no!" My father shouted "This (MF) done kill my dog!" First time I had ever heard Daddy claim ownership of our dog! He was mad! Damn mad! The man took the papers up, looked at them said, yes sir, your dog was uncontrollable, vicious, dangerous. "Sir, my ass, dangerous, he was protecting his yard, his home. You people killed him, you dirty sons of bitches killed him. Where is he?" My father was out of the pocket, mad, angry and most of all hurt! Super hurt! I just stood there shocked.

The office was quiet, time seemed to stand still. Several people that were there also to pick up their animals just stood silent, feeling my dad's pain. He picked the papers back up the dog catcher man had put down and slowly walked out of the door. That was the longest walk back home. Daddy threw the choker chain he had with him off the pier where the Port Welcome was parked (a favorite cruise ship for black people to party on).

As we struck the bottom of Pennsylvania Avenue and Greene Street downtown, we stopped at the liquor store. Daddy got a pint of Big Apple wine, drank it straight down. We walked on stopping five more times at liquor stores to get pints of wine, then a ½ pint of Gin. I just watched him turn them up and bring them down right outside of the stores' front doors. He was destroyed by the dog's death (murder) he kept saying, "Killed". He died like a dog! Now, I'll tell you Daddy didn't like this dog to hear him tell it, he was a mutt, a soup bone, good for nothing, not even good for the seasoning beans, "But was alright with him". That's what Daddy would say, all drunked up upon seeing him, wagging his tail, glad to see him back home after being gone all day. Daddy would share his food with him, even candy and cake and cookies, ice cream, crabs, fish, anything. He would curse the dog out if he looked like he was going to cock his leg to mark an area in the kitchen after Daddy would let him in so he could cuss the poor dog out. They were buddies for real. During the summer, Daddy would have the dog laid out pulling ticks off of him. Then laugh like hell as he put coal oil on him to clear the ticks and fleas that hold on. As the dog ran back and forth, trying to dislodge the burning liquid off himself, then to fight like hell with my father not to take a bath to wash the remaining coal oil off him. Plus they were drinking buddies. I had seen him giving Blackie hits of wine to loosen up from time to time during the winter, stating "This will keep "Brother Arthur" from kicking in on you son-son." Yea, they were tight! But this was too much!

When we got back to the house, Dad took up his seat by the living room window and I heard him crying! It messed me up. The man had started out sober and ended up drunk with his dog, his friend dead. I felt like a piece of shit but I carried my feelings inside but it hurt, Old Blackie gone. Later that night Cuz hollered from the back alley. My father's room was on the back, he heard him and called me. As I was going to the bathroom window to holler back, my father said you and Frances' boy are both going to end up in jail. I didn't know that Daddy knew Cuz, he had never said anything about Cuz all of this time. It was like he didn't know of him or even saw us together, ever. Daddy knew more than I ever knew, sober or drunk he was on to me.

I went out back. Cuz and I sat under the streetlight as I filled him in on the past two days and it's happenings. He knew the highlights of the raid (search) but not about the stash of money and the dog. We disagreed about the new shop area and agreed to work from the Avenue near the phone booth and our favorite perch, a pair of steps. We used to watch what was happening on the Avenue, 2675 Pennsylvania Avenue, with a view of everything and all of those bus lines. Yes, our new but old job site. The day and nights went on. We sold our wares, but Cuz still doing the school thing, me, laying around all day doing sales, bored again.

Now, Cuz had an age card he had gotten from somebody. It made it easy to get into the pool rooms. I didn't have one, so I got one also. This was my new outlet plus no more pissing in the alleys and I could play a game or two of pool. From time to time I would go into the pool hall known almost all of these dudes, but not known for shooting any pool. The houseman would hit me right off with no hanging around. This place is to play pool. Well, (you ain't said nothing) I'd reply. Now, I was a Boy's Police Club brat. I had a badge since I was 8 years old and no stranger to a pool table by a long shot. At the club if you lost a game of pool once you got on, it would be a month before you got back on it to play again. So let one of these niggers think they had something easy to pick on. In a while I was a regular with a "rep", not scared to get, could shoot, but could cut the shit out of a ball, but would get kind of wild once I went to the shit house once or twice (fucking with that shit), you might win some of his money. But, they wouldn't just jump without thinking first to see how I was acting or if I had Cuz with me to keep me under control because I would fight a nigger in a heart beat (no question).

The pool room afforded us a new place to deal also, especially if it rained or was cold outside. Also knowing money came in and out of the place. But you couldn't deal in the place or that was said to be the rule anyhow. Thanks for the age card. During the day I would hang between outside, inside, make my walks around the neighborhood selling our wares. All was going well once again. Also, I had met some real hustlers, thieves, businessmen, the works and had also been noticed by a lot of people who liked Cuz's and my little hustling ability. They were begging to come at us. I began to know a lot of men, surprisingly a lot of them were more than they appeared to be. The background of some of these guys was awesome. Yes, there were some who had jail time behind them, stories of killing, robbing, thieves, pimps and the like. When doctors, lawyers, landlords, number writers, businessmen, even teachers, dentists, and funeral directors played pool, they would get into me, question after question but they made their questions always on a cool tip, smooth with the ways and how do you feel about this and that young man? And what do you want out of life son? The same reply I would give was to be rich, not to have to want for nothing by the age of 45 years old, and be retired. I always got that chuckle and a smile, and most times the conversation would end there. Then I would just wait to see if I got a kick back to my answer.

Most times Cuz would tell me all of the play he would get, because he had a calm, slick way about him and the old men went for it and he wore this stingy brim black felt hat called a playboy with a little feather on it and a toothpick hanging out the side of his mouth, clean as a pin, never saying a word unless you said something to him. They dug it and we played it up for the big black nigger sitting quietly always nearby was his stickman and they knew how I could get off. So, the two of us made an awesome team.

Well, the newspapers were talking about this war going on in some place called Viet Nam and something about a draft. It didn't mean anything to us. We thought things were beginning to get a little strained between Cuz and me because I was hitting the junk harder than ever. Being involved with this new group, I had met a new group of young dudes, dropouts, losers, and a few hardcore junkies, old and young. We talked about my drug usage but I did what I wanted to, plus I thought it was me who put the most time on the job. Cuz was doing the school thing. One of the old guys dug me, he was a barber at one the hippest barber shops on Pennsylvania Avenue where anyone who was somebody or wanted to be somebody got their hair cut. This man had one terrible pool talent. He could shoot some pool. When he was shooting, I would be sitting ringside watching his every move, position pool man perfect. He had seen me watching him often. Then one day, I was playing a dude. I went to the shit house to piss. He walked in and said you can beat that man (you have to think the last ball you shoot carries the same weight, that the first ball you shoot, either one can cost you the game). Man, this was awesome, I thought about that all the way back to the table. I beat the man out of $300.00 that night. I even tried to hit the tipster off with a $20.00 bill and offered to buy him a ½ pint of any drink he wanted. He refused the money but accepted the ½ pint. He got some Brandy, Brandy? I stated yea, he said with a smile. That's my namesake, Brandy, I love them he stated. Later, I found out the name was his nickname for a different reason, it was given to him because the chicks loved this dude. Shortly we were tight. I was practicing pool shots, playing games for sodas, ½ pints of liquor, and submarine sandwiches and smokes. I was learning how to win money at pool but most of all how to win under pressure no matter what the stakes were.

    Brandy was like a big brother, he took me under his wing. Now, I knew he was a barber but he was too clean, too cool, and a lot of these guys were like leery of him. I found out he had killed a guy when he was younger and had learned to cut hair while in the joint and being red and pretty, he didn't have it easy doing his bit. He had to prove himself and he did, also he had tried some light pimping for a while, so that's why he had such a soft name like Brandy. Ahh huh! So, I figured I could learn a lot from this man, and I did. What my man did and said I paid plenty attention to. I began to steal some of his style, he started to cut my hair and trim my light mustache that was coming in about now. But Brandy let me in on a big secret, at night the man the pool hustler, ex-pimp, this cool dude worked! Yes, worked 11 p.m. to 7:30 a.m. at a can manufacturing company. He explained to me only a fool would try to beat the man ducking the jailhouse on a full time basis. You have to have a hold card. This was the second time he had blown me away. I couldn't wait to tell Cuz about this dude because we both dug him. Brandy did what he called teaching me to think like a thinking man. To think about having a wife, kids, the house, bank accounts, credit, respect, and a future. "You need and gotta have a job." Boy! He said this with a lot of conviction. We talked many a day about the advantages of that statement and it made plenty of sense to me. I liked it! I really did.

In fact, I asked Aunt Corrine to ask Mr. Brooks, her boss at the restaurant to allow me to come back to work, but I need a little more money than before, plus I had my GED you know. Mr. Brooks took me back, less time I was on the corner, less time in the pool hall. It had to be noticed. There was still drugs to be found that we had out there but you would cop from one of my homeboys or wait for Cuz to get out of school or for me to get off one of those buses after work. This was good for me, my habit slacked off because I was working and no way was my aunt going to catch me high and I was missing from the scene on the block from the police, plus still getting paid.

One Saturday night, Brandy pulled me out of the poolroom, saying he wanted me to take a ride with him, ok. But I still questioned where to, he said "Just ride will you?" We drove towards downtown, past the Harbor, then over to the east side of town. We went way over to where all the factories were located. He stopped in front of this building where all of these cars were being parked , men going into the yard gate. Brandy jumped out of the car, leaned back inside. He then opened the window on the driver's side and said "Come pick me up by 7:45 a.m." I said "7:45 a.m., what?" "Yea, he said 7:45 a.m. tomorrow morning, you heard me." Blown away again! He was leaving me with his "HOG" YEA! It wasn't stolen, I have a license and money in my pockets, Saturday night, wait? Oh yea, plenty of gas! A "HOG" I turned that radio up a couple of notches, hit the gas and started to coast by everybody, driving like this Cadillac belonged to me, young, rich and slick.

When I hit the 2700 block of Pennsylvania Avenue and stepped out of that pretty sky blue with white hard top with $100.00 top of the line gold fern vein tires on it "HOG". I was the shit! Everyone knew whose car it really belonged to, but he had trusted me with his "HOG"! They knew I was his shorty, no doubt! I parked and went to find Cuz. I was told Cuz had left the top of the hill, he had gone to see his girl. Ok, I thought I have to show off this car. I had to put some blue threads on to match this ride. So I jumped around to the house to change clothes. I threw some water on myself. I put on some Ole Spice and lit out .

I picked up my load. Started it up, making sure everyone saw me, pulled off slowly, nodding as I passed all of the opened mouths. Cuz was over his new girl's house, a fine red bone named Stella Brown. She worked part time at the ice cream shop down the street from one of the poolrooms facing the Avenue. Cuz, I know was falling in love. He had slacked off on the hustle, wasn't talking nor trying to jump any of the other home girls, even the ones who wanted to be jumped. He was eating a lot of ice cream and chocolate cake they sold at the eatery. Plus, he was in my case about getting high. He was changing. At time I would be looking for him, just to see him jumping in a cab heading south, yea, he was strung for sure. But, I thought once he had scored, he would be back on point. Even that night I had the "HOG", Cuz had taken a walk with his girl and had not gotten to show the "HOG" off. Soon, it was to come to past, Cuz and me would stray away from one another, because the writing was on the wall. One night on a weekend for some reason Cuz and I were sitting on the steps at 2675 Pennsylvania Avenue at Clifton looking out over the block. We talked about 20 – 25 years from that day what and where we wanted to be, it was one of those heart to heart talks. Cuz to Cuz. In a lot of ways, we wanted the same things but the time limit was short of my dreams of retirement, but I didn't mention that. But, we painted a grand picture, all positive. Then we went home feeling good about ourselves.

The following weekend for the first time Cuz asked me what did I get from being high all the time. I could not really answer, but I did say you should try it. Since he didn't get high, I suggested that he take pills. I didn't want to hurt my cousin first time out of the chute. We popped a few pills or should I say I popped 4 pills, he did 2 pills and then we got 2 cups of coffee to speed the effects up. The pills hit, we were high! Cuz was torn up, stumbling around, off balance, sweating and stuff. Well, we had to get away.

People had never seen him like that and they damn sure wasn't going to, so we left the area. Cuz didn't like this (shit), he kept on saying, "No, I don't like this at all! I feel funny!" He complained for hours seemed like. Then Cuz stumbled, almost fell on his face, he caught himself but had scraped his shoes, he had scraped his gators or were they lizards. This put the nail in the coffin. All of a sudden he seemed (sober) cold sober, looking down at his shoes shaking his head "No!" He stated, "Not for me!"

We stopped walking together after that night. We would always remain buds, cousins, friends but it was over. This world had been blown apart. I took it hard, like this was my man, my strength where I was weak. He was my back up, hustling buddy. But I was told that's how life goes. One thing I didn't have any insight to was when Cuz and I stopped walking together things would change. The re-ups for drugs slacked up. Some of the old men didn't pull me up as they had been doing. The money was getting slow. It took Brandy to hip me, that they didn't want to (f) with me too tough because I was a (Hype) a (Hype). I didn't consider myself to be a junkie! This hit like a ton of bricks! A junkie, like I didn't even think like that, or carry myself like a junkie! I had the shit, sold it, I had money! The more he talked I realized I was strung, a junkie! He then told me to get it together or he too was going to cut me loose saying if your boy, your people threw you away, what do you think you are worth?

My world seemed to have gotten smaller and lonelier. I put down some hard thinking. I was talking with one of the older guys and he hipped me to something called treatment (Meth) Methadone. It craves the need to do dope. It's free, just go to a class once week, you can get your self straight in a couple of months. Plus you have doctors and nurses to help with anything else you may have wrong with you. I went for it, I signed up on the (Gram) Program but (Gram) called by all of the Hypes I had come to admit I liked being high. I liked the feeling and all that went with it. But I had to kick the 90 day program at 30 milligrams, was the offering. I jumped on it. I worked the routine to the letter, ducking all of the temptations to re-use. I would hit and run, drink my dose and get out of dodge, make my group session and dash. There were no take home dosages so one had to do seven days a week as many of the things I've gotten involved in I worked hard to do it well.

With only one week to go to completion of my 90 days, I had just come up to the hill from the program, walked into the pool room, played a practice game of pool. I wanted a sweet potato pie from the Blue Room Restaurant across the street. As I was crossing the street, I saw a couple of dudes over at Brandy's car, now knowing there was a third party inside of the "HOG". As I walked over one of them knocked on the car body and one of my close homeboys got out of the ride, shutting the door behind himself. I messed up before I can say a word, he speaks, "Say black, I know how this looks, but a hustle is a hustle". I looked down at his side, there is a dark brown duffle looking bag, stepping backward, the other guys closed ranks to block my path. "Homes said you know how it is man," then shuffled backwards and started to slow trot off in the opposite direction. Now, this scene had not gone unnoticed. Someone yelled to Brandy, his car was being taken off. He was coming with blood in his eyes. The two blockers broke and was burning sidewalk up getting away. Brandy confronts me. "What were those niggers doing huh?" He saw the latch was up on the door, opened it and cursed! "Who did this? Who took my shit? What's their names, I'll kill the (MFs)." "Who are they," he was hot! Smoking! Now, I couldn't tell! I knew them. I have talked to them! They took off my man, took his stuff, but there was a code. I couldn't snitch, I had all of the old men, the young guys, the Hypes, the chicks looking on. All of us had done something wrong, all of us probably stole something at one time or another and if you got away with it, oh well, but to ask someone to snitch on another hustler. I couldn't do it. Not even for Brandy. I just walked away from the scene.

Brandy hung around until late that night offering money to find out who the robbers were, but got no takers, not even any of the Hypes tried to cash in. Word was my man was through with me. I had thrown him away for a couple of Hypes. Just like my junkie ass self. Brandy disappeared. I haven't seen him since. Seems anybody I got tight with was finding a reason to kick me to the curb. Everybody seemed like they were talking about what had come off, so I felt it was time to find new backers, a new source to cop from along with my man that was hitting me off all along. I was going to hang downtown. Yes, down the bottom of the Avenue, the bottom of Pennsylvania

Avenue where it was really happening (down the way). I had no idea that separation from people I dug was part of the reason I was on a road to destroying my life. I was just reacting, trying to recover from situations in the only way I knew how, fuck it, carry on. I would be rich and retired one day with no worries. My life was seemingly to get more complicated.

    My mother was about to make a move from down the way to a better area of town some 25 blocks from where the kids had known as their second home. They were all excited, I had mixed feelings about the move, most of our relatives lived down the way and I had made plans on opening a new shop knowing I would be in touch with *Ma* and the kids on a daily basis. Oh well, that went right out the window. Plans were made and plans were going into action no matter what, was the way I looked at it. Now cutting into a new area and new mobs wasn't going to be easy and I knew this. To boot, I didn't have Cuz to watch my back for he was known by a lot of young men and old heads on this end of town. I missed him on a lot of fronts (for sure).

    This cutting in was going to take finesse, thinking I would slide into one of the groups of a few of the guys I knew was working and needed some help getting re-up because some crew worker had messed up the money or ran off with part of a package, or the stash got stolen or ripped off by stick up men it would be best for me to come aboard saving the day with cash money to bring on the re-up. Then I could not only blend in but be a boss at the same time. I had also thought of getting part of a package on consignment, but then I would have to get a crew and fight for a corner or block to work from. Too much drama to that plus I could get croaked, too many outlaws and players out there to think that way or I could get some weed and play the middle and work out of my pocket and sell the bosses and workers weed and work my way into where I wanted. Yea, weed, that's where I had got my start with Cuz and it worked, could work again. This plan sounded good to me, and I wouldn't have a habit nor could I get strung on weed. I would keep my head on straight. I got a hit with some good herb but the action was going towards the harder stuff or that's how I saw it. The projects were just a few blocks from my mother's old house and I would stroll down that way selling my herbs.

One of my friends from up top swung down on this end of town. I knew, he also had one huge newspaper route that this area was his bread and butter also expected he was working for a man that had put him down with some killer dope. He was hitting and I had stumbled on to just what I was looking for, a buddy, a partner, a homeboy. Well, Hello. Now Bunky was seasoned, his plans of what he wanted and how he was going to get it had been in the works for some time. He was serious. Bunky was schooling, throwing papers, flipping dope, shooting dope, and a member of a tough crew! Plus, he lived on top of the hill with me. It didn't take much for us to get tight. He knew me, and me him.

We would walk home after working at the projects, stop at the Chinese joint, get rice and gravy or he would get shrimp and rice and I would get green pepper pork and rice and slow walk, talking and dreaming how rich we were going to be some day. Time passed and Bunky and me came to be the same as Cuz and me. I knew all of his moves, knew damn near all of his contacts. But one who he was getting down from, we would share everything and hang tough, but we also shot plenty of drugs. He loved drugs, he had used up damn nearly all of his veins and he was as young as me, but he had discipline about how he would do drugs. Only after work and only do the best drugs. Even it if meant going miles to get them. We wouldn't do our drugs if they were not up to par. We would ride, walk, wait hours for whoever had the hook up, to show up and buy spoons of raw dope to do ourselves. Top shelf always Man! I would be fed up for real, asleep but dead awake. Higher than a kite. We had clothes, money and girls. Bunky had introduced me to chicks, chicks that would do anything for drugs and we used them up, some times I would be so high, I didn't even want any, thinking they would blow my high with all of the bullshit they could sometime bring once they got high. Then at other times I wanted to try 2 and 3 at a time (that must have been the drugs talking to me). Well, without saying the job over at the restaurant was out of the picture, I wasn't going home most nights, too high to go in plus Aunt Corrine and Daddy were there and no way was I going to go to my mother's with that shit.

    I stayed at girls' houses, and sometimes worked all night (open shop) dust 'til dawn. Yes, we did, hustling at night was different, you couldn't see much. You had to be on the look out for the police, knockers, stick-up men, and clients trying to get over and creepers trying to steal your stash. They were everywhere. At night you didn't want the drugs on you, too risky, you could get taken off, robbed or killed. Naw! Not in your pocket! Candy bags, potato chip bags, under cars, under bricks, cracks in the walls, trash cans, anywhere.

    One had to find a sharpness, a 6th sense about how someone walked up to be served, how they gave you eye contact, their body movement, but most of all if or if not to pull the iron we had close at hand at all times. During those nights out there and most of the time everybody knew of us being strapped because we grand stand as soon as we would hit the block acting like we were going to hurt someone for one reason or another. Word would get out, you were strapped if anybody knew of it (for sure) plus there was plenty of watchers, watching and waiting to make their move if they got the chance. Like this chump came to cop one day, he had ran off with this guy's money at one time, the dude caught sight of him, crept up on him and like to took his head off. That fool was screaming and howling bloody murder and not one soul raised an eyebrow (as you do you get done).

I heard someone say this kind of happening went on all of the time. People would catch their buddies, so called friends trying to switch needles they had filled with water to beat one another for their drugs, or switch dope bags with dummy bags they had made up with flour, baby powder, Standback headache powder, anything white that would dissolve in water when heated. Yes, things could really get dirty in this game. So one had to be on point at all times. Bunky had some funny ways, he didn't believe in taking short money from anyone, not $.25 short. Saying if we got caught the judge wasn't going to give us any less time for doing anyone any favors. So get straight money for straight dope. It made sense, even though I always thought sell it just to get rid of that shit.

Then my buddy was told his brother-in-law had a job for him with the City, the City with benefits, holidays paid, vacation, sick leave, the credit union. Well, how could anyone say no to that. The City, one could look forward to working easy and it took off any pressure of getting fired. Nobody ever got fired from a City job. Well, he jumped right on it! Now we knew we could always keep a package with this extra money coming in or should I say that Herb had coming in, he was about to make $5.00 an hour pay, that was good money. Just as we planned, things got easier, we re-upped like clock work, his half and mine. I still had cash stashed cause I always said I would never be caught broke.

We came up with a new plan since we worked a lot of nights because Bunky's shift didn't really start until he got off from work. I would lay to watch his back and serve a little if things really picked up. We went to the surplus store and got some black sweatshirts and black work pants and work caps and bucket hats. Also, since blue jeans were cheap, we got several pairs of blue jeans and blue jean wrangler jackets. These outfits were our main outfits of choice for damn near 15 years. All of the fancy clothes and slick shoes and coats were not worn by us and damn near any other hustler on the west side of B-more (Baltimore).

  Once the blue jeans and Lee and Wrangler gear caught on, everybody was wearing them, and man when they came out with the black colored ones stores couldn't keep them in stock. But I must give credit to one of our buddies. He was a karate fighter, he liked the look, started wearing it, then his club members did also and seemingly the entire West side followed and made it a style. Thanks to Dave and Richard. Well, Bunky and I worked our thing. Just like real businessmen, me working on the top of Pennsylvania Avenue, 2700 block from 8:00 a.m. to 4:30 p.m., then meet Bunky after he got off. We would walk down the way, he would start by 5:00 pm until we turned in (no telling) but no matter what time, he still went to work on his good city job.

  Often, we would stay up all night but we would hang out at the Arcade that stayed open all night right next to a strip joint, Les Gal's. The place was tight! We reaped the benefits of the action that went on inside the place. Truly, we liked their customers and they liked our products. A very good relationship we maintained with very little hassle from the police. There I met a mentor to Bunky and I learned a few things from him. Also, along the way Money was cool. Yes, Money was his name. He worked, had a family, was our elder and was cool and fair. But most of all was a good model of how to hustle and carry on a life at the same time was what he showed me, I liked his style and imitated it in days to come. Brandy, Big Boy and a host of others will teach me as time goes on (believe me). All along life was going on in the world because it wasn't all about us.

There was a war going on in Viet Nam and the USA, we were warming up to kick some butt, and the USA had started a draft! I was 17 ½ years old and had to go get registration cards at the Custom House in my town. So, I did. What the hell? I wouldn't be 18 until March of the year coming in, plus they didn't want me anyhow. I had been in jail four times, car theft, battery, assault, disorderly, plus probation, no worry. Oh yea, and several overnight stays for getting caught in poolroom raids for gambling and drug raids.

It was good being a juvenile at times, but this 18 and war was something to think about. Oh yea, I forgot the nuisance house charge also and pissing in the alley charges and open containers too. Well, you know, they shouldn't want me, not me? But come March 11, plus 10 more days I get draft papers and a number 313. When they laid that letter on me! I just couldn't believe it. I was shocked but pleased! Yes, pleased. Why, because my father had told me about overseas, my uncle had told me about overseas. I had heard all of the old men talk about Korea, Dominican Republic, Philippines, France, Germany, Africa, Guam, the girls, the beautiful places, the good times they shared with other GIs. But my father after hearing of the draft papers and numbers, this had given him new life.

Daddy spent hours upon hours, even waking me up at 6:00 a.m. in the morning, man sometimes I had just laid down trying to catch 60 winks, "Boy put your feet on the floor. Get ready for it," he would bellow. Obediently I would, my head bad from drugging all day and all night long, he didn't care and liked what I was doing less I knew that fact. Big Spoonhead as his buddies called him and they called me Little Spoon, which made me feel special because his buddy knew the real man he was and I was told Daddy had a hell of a past. Quite the young man he was, respected and loved by the ladies, plus very good with a knife when it came to a fight. Most of his war talks were mostly about the land, the beautiful area he had seen, how different the people were but how much they were just plain ole people. Being a truck driver overseas, Daddy did a lot of traveling in Korea and we stayed in this set of encyclopedias we had with him pointing out parts of that country he had traveled. He had a way of making our time together come to life for me. I wanted to experience that same feeling. I also was getting some feedback about the war I was about to face. Some of the older homeboys from the top of the hill were coming home from this war in Viet Nam.

The stories they told were different from my father's. Most were of hardships, wet or extra hot weather, nowhere to hide, or there was too much jungle to even know where and who was trying to knock you off. Men were dying terrible deaths, men crying, crying real tears about a buddy dying. Some of the homeys left alive and we went to or heard about their funerals and television painted an ugly story about this war. It was like the Big Picture, a television show about World War II. This was something to think about. But if my number came up, I was expected to go. I was ready to do my do. My father did it, my uncles did it so now it was going to be my time. So! My focus was scattered at this time. I don't know if I should clean up because I was told the Army gave a physical test.

My people wanted me to go into the service, Army, Navy or Marines, which one to choose? What do I want to do, be in the war? How long will I sign up for? See, I know nothing about what's going on. Just so happen one of my older returning Viet Nam homeboy Veteran pulled me up, oh wait a minute! I forgot to say when I got my draft papers damn nearly everybody I knew the same age group as me, got their draft papers and numbers. Everyone in the neighborhood was in an uproar (I meant to say that). Well, anyway, my homeboy pulled me up in the poolroom stating, "Little nigger, Nam will straighten you out, Dusty. It's just what you and a lot of you little niggers need, that's if you don't get wiped out." He wasn't saying it to be shitty or anything he was a cool egg, liked by everybody. I knew who knew him, Boo Boo was his name-- said to look a lot like he could have been related to me; but he wasn't. I know because I asked my father about that very thing. "Daddy is Boo Boo related to us?" Is the way that went. "No", was the answer. That's Stanley's boy. I was fine with that, but Boo Boo would have a step full of us young boys listening to him talk about Viet Nam and his experiences over there, a great source of information he was. I took everything he said to heart. I tired to clean up a little. I got on a program drinking Methadone, 30 milligrams on a 30 day program. For the first time in a long time, I was trying to go half way straight. I looked forward to seeing Boo Boo and talking about the war. Slowing my roll with the drugs on all fronts, I tried to stay close to the house.

My Aunt and father must have thought I was on the run, hiding out from someone or something they had not seen this much of me in years. I even watched television with my father, Superman, Cisco Kid, Hop Along Cassidy, Alfred Hitchcock, the works. Yea, I had got grounded again. Bunky didn't press me, he carried on as usual. I missed the action, but I was doing the program. But I was doing a lot of thinking. I heard a lot about Nam. The things that stuck in my mind most was the sunshine, the rich earth, the Weed, the golden triangle, the dope that was coming down some trail, it was supposed to be 100% pure horse, uncut, tons and tons of Heroin and GIs could get it on the streets over there and you smoked it. Yea, smoked it, just that pure. A lot of soldiers were getting a lot at home and getting rich. Well, Well, why not me. I could do that so my ear was to the ground listening to hear all I could about Nam. <u>Look</u>, <u>Time</u>, and all of the magazines had articles on Nam every day. Some of the pictures were grizzly, dead bodies, bombed buildings, wounded soldiers, the works, but no talk about the drugs, but the returning Vets talked plenty about the junk. A lot of the returning Vets were all fucked up, crazy as hell, out of the pocket, changed men, some wore that jungle outfit every day and seemed spaced out, lost.

    The dope must have been awesome. I thought, yea it will sell good over here! I got to test some shit, a Thai stick one afternoon while in the pool room. One of the fellows had bought this big, long cigar looking thing, called it a Thai stick, said it came from Nam. It was soaked in heroin or Mary Jane. This was the first time I had heard of Mary Jane. We called it gangster, weed, reefer, marijuana, hemp, rope, loco weed, anyhow, I got to pull up on this stogee. First!, the room turned golden, golden yellow, bright as the sun, the music that was playing on the jukebox seemed to drag, very slow, it sounded like dogs howling. The people shooting pool started to move in slow motion, the air around me got heavy. I looked out of the window behind me. I could see heat streamers coming up off the sidewalk. I could almost see through this girl's summer sundress to the form of her shapely body framed, looked extra good! Then there was like a tick or something, then everything was normal, normal speed only to happen again into slow motion. Man this was boss! The in and out feeling was too much, no needles, no blood, no top or spoon, just one match to light up and blow. I must have set in that one seat for about four hours torn up and loving every minute of it. The way the balls rolled around the pool table, the players' faces, their expression, their emotions when they missed a shot was most entertaining. I really enjoyed myself more and more. I was looking forward to going to Viet Nam.

    With all of the stuff I had going on in my head I had to air out, so I came upon a 1964 Chevy Impala, blue with white interior. Just so happen it had a coin slot ignition. It was not in the lock position sitting there waiting for me to take it for a drive. Now, I hadn't stolen a car in years, but it was too good to pass up. So, I combed the nearby alleys looking for some wire. I found the wire, popped the window lock, took the ride. It was nice, an automatic that was cool. I had a $5.00 bag of Herb and a pack of top rolling papers and a box of stick matches and ¾ tank of gas and away I went.

I cruised for about half of an hour, blown away, the radio was on, the four speakers kicking, the Quiet Storm with DJ Major Davis was just about to start his show. Now, I had to have someone to share this ride, this time with and I was never choosey who this chick named Tammy, young, sweet but a mama's girl. She was who I wanted to share this night with, but how? I would need help pulling her out of the block and even more help to get her to get into this stolen ride and cruise with me. Tammy was a girlfriend to all of my sisters and I knew my sisters loved me. They would pull her in, cover her and me and with a little convincing may be even cruise a little. This was the weed talking, wow! Yea, I had it all figured out. Well, it didn't come off. I found myself cruising alright, but with a bunch of hardheads, all loud, dum-dum blowouts, blowing my high and demanding to go faster and faster! Well, I ditched them, got $3.00 worth of gas and took off up I-83.

It was just DJ Major Davis and me and that 1964 Chevy with miles and miles of road ahead. I drove up to York, PA, stopped at a truck stop got an egg omelet, with a side of scrapple and pineapple juice, a $3.00 meal, then coasted back down I-83 to B-more. That ride I carried through my whole tour of Nam whenever I got depressed looking up at the night skies over in Southeast Asia. That was one awesome ride in someone else's car, "a cool 1964 Chevy." I did right by the owner, I parked the car dead in the middle of the street, on one of Baltimore's known business street, then walked off knowing the police would get a call about it being left there. I wiped it down real good, I was high, not crazy or stuck on dumb, fingerprints you know. I was as usual mindless of any harm I may have done for once done, it was over with and that was that. But a lesson of life's up's and downs and consequences of what you do tend to catch up with you, it was about to hit me right in the face.

My father sat in the house for two straight weeks. He was just sitting in his chair in the kitchen at the window near the sink, or in his chair at the window that was his domain. I asked him why he had shut himself in the house for so long? "I'm blind. I can't see, my eyesight is knocked out son." I didn't know what to say. I just stood there, then I looked around for help. Should I run up to my mother's house to tell her, no can't do that. She is in that nursing class, Aunt Corrine is at work, Cuz ain't around. Just me and the quietness of the house. I flopped down on the sofa, wasted! All kinds of stuff was running wild in my mind, blind, can't see, all of blackness. I was more scared for him than he seemed to be. Daddy sat there, head turned towards the window. I sat looking at him trying to hold back tears that filled my eye sockets. Later that day Aunt Corrine came home. I told her about what I knew. After telling her, out I went to get ripped. Yes, I messed up. All that good time I put in not shooting junk, but I was not forgetting my ole man while out there I was asking around about Veterans, benefits, the VA cause daddy was a Vet.

Once the word was out, the old men in the neighborhood were tearing the front door down to see my old man. I didn't know he was liked that much, Longshoremen were coming pass with food, leaving money, and just sitting with daddy talking shit. But one man came over, Mr. Greentree. Mr. Greentree owned the stable with horses and wagons up off of Pennsylvania

Avenue. All of the Arabs (vendors of fruits and vegetables) came on Fridays. Arabs, men a hold over from the 1940's and 1950's are unique to Baltimore giving one a taste of the old south, served black people long before supermarkets were a lifesaver for black poor people. They gave pay day food loans to the housewives and widows were greeted like family. Plus some Arabs would bring the horses out on Sundays to sell pony rides to the kids. Most of my buddies could ride like the Cisco Kid or Roy Rogers.

Mr. Greentree and my father were boyhood friends, they had even did time in the joint three times and unknown to me until then he had daddy's dog Buster housed at the stable. I thought the dog was dead long ago, because Buster was crazy, he was a fighter, a Pit fighter known by all of the sporting men up and down the east coast and up state PA, NY, OH, CT, he was known. But since daddy had all of us kids, Buster had to go once he got blooded (killed a couple of dogs in matches), he couldn't be trusted so Mr. Greentree housed him at his stable. Truthfully, it gave the stable a lot of static having Buster living there. Plus, the money Daddy and Mr. Greentree made off of the puppies Buster fathered was good money.

Mr. Greentree with his big three hundred and some pounds would sit and sit all day. Some days he would keep my father laughing. Mr. Greentree, me and daddy all went to Marine Hospital in Baltimore to get Daddy tested for his sight, then to Perry Point Medical Veterans Hospital for Daddy's training for the blind. Mr. Greentree was a real good model to learn how to be a true friend. Now being a man of the world, he knew that I was on something and he often spoke on that subject but added (just like talking to a stone wall) upon closing often and that's how I took it.

Anyway, he hung tough and for that I'll always be thankful to his memory. He died of a heart attack shortly before I went into the Army. R.I.P. Mr. Greentree. Remember now I am back on heroin once again. I had again got a small package but it was a good product, but I stayed close to the house. I was checking on daddy all day long, since he was there all day long. Daddy and I even sat in the sun on the front steps and the back porch and we talked a bunch. I learned more about him. Man, it was, it was great! Daddy told me a lot of personal stuff about him and Mama, his early days. It seemed Daddy was getting me to know all about himself all at once. I remember him insisting Noddie (my brother) and myself almost being ordered to sit and listen to him talk. Daddy even requested me to get my sisters to come up to the house for breakfast to eat with him. He just wanted their company.

 Well, I did my daily thing, handling my business and the business of getting high. Then, I got the dreaded letter of notice that I was drafted. My number was up, 313 had been included in the draft. It was even published in the newspapers. Yea, I was to go to Nam, no doubt! My mind set now was to get ready for the big day. The dope I was selling was alright, but not good enough to stand up for a month hold over. I had to get a few spoons of *raw*, something that would at least take a 25 cut. Now, this was not to be sold to the locals, this was to be carried with me when I left. I knew I would still have a yearn for weeks, may be even a couple of months while away from home and I would or may not could cop so I was going to have a stash, a rainy day package on hand and may be I would flip some of it. So, now I was looking and I was dead serious to find some good shit! Searching for raw was a real trip. Well, I did cop. Now, what came off next kicked me right out of the box.

 As it had come to be commonplace, my father was talking about himself and what had happened to him overseas. It was a Saturday night. I had made plans to go the dance hall, the Crystal Ballroom in East Baltimore. My homeboys also were getting prepared to go. I took my bath and danced around the room the radio blasting out the

Four Tops ("Bernadette"). I put my clothes on, slipped on my "Gators", greased my nappy bush and was ready to check out. My Dad was already in bed in the back room. I gave notice as I was leaving ("Dad, I'm gone"). I swear I heard him reply. Down the steps I went, out the door, my aunt and three of her girlfriends were two doors down from our house. I walked down to say I was going. My aunt asked me had my father ate yet? I replied I thought he had eaten by this time. She stated he didn't come down to dinner, but she was going to get him to eat something. We both walked back to the house where I took my leave. I turned the corner and started down the block ¾ down the block, I heard someone calling me, then whoever called again. I stopped and walked back up the street. There I saw one of my aunt's girlfriends, Mrs. Tate, who lived two doors to the right of our house. Mrs. Tate said babe your aunt wants you to come right back to the house, being obedient, I did.

In the house I went, but it seemed dark, dark like there was a 25 watt light bulb on. Nobody was downstairs. Man, it looked even darker up there than it did where I was standing. I slowly climbed the stairs. I entered the middle room, my room. My aunt was sitting on my bed, her head hung down in her chest not saying a word. Mrs. Tate now, standing behind me said, "I'm sorry babe," I had no idea what the hell was going on. I started to walk towards the back room.

The room was pitch black, a faint glow of light seemed to part the darkness. The closer and closer I got to Daddy, laying there asleep. I reached out to touch him to wake him up to get some food, to eat. I touched his feet saying "Daddy, Daddy." He felt like ice cubes, his feet were hard, and cold. My eyes roamed upwards towards his chest, neck, then face. Oh, my God! Daddy's face was screwed up, ugly, scary! This wasn't my father! No! I couldn't move!

All kinds of thoughts were going while in my head. I had just talked with him, he had just talked with me about himself and my mother! He had just had breakfast with my brothers and sisters. He was just smiling, talking, walking, breathing, alive. No, Daddy ain't dead, not really dead! I never thought Daddy would die. Not die without telling me. I didn't expect this! I didn't get to say goodbye, nobody was going to get to say goodbye. When I could move, when I could hear again, I heard my aunt crying in the middle room. It seemed to be blazing hot in the room. I could see better in the dark light, fear had passed. I stood there looking at my dead father. Then for some reason all I could do was to sit aside him and I began to hug him. I wanted to make his cold body warm again. I told him I loved him and held him tightly, seemingly a slight breeze blew in the window. My aunt came into the room Mrs. Tate, also. Someone said we have got to contact Delores.

Upon hearing my mother's name, I wondered how to tell her, but I sprung up and almost ran out of the room saying I'll be right back. I rushed pass Mrs. Tate and Aunt Corrine, down the stairs, down the hallway out the door. The front was crowded with neighbors and onlookers. I booked up the block running to my mother's house. I was burning those Gators up along the way. This hard core, hardheaded cried. I couldn't hold it in, trying to get myself together as I closed in on my mother's house. Once there, I went in to the back yard way. Mama's kitchen light was on. I could see someone standing and someone sitting in a chair. The closer I got, I knew that was my cousin, Shirley, Cuz's oldest sister. She was doing my mother's hair. I stopped short of the door, catching my breath, turned the doorknob and entered. I spoke to the both of them, then went on to say Mama, Daddy is dead. My mother screamed, Shirley reared in shock, then silence. Then *Ma* spoke, "Obie, get my purse". Off we went, back to 2618 Woodbrook and Daddy.

Upon reaching the house, *Ma* went right upstairs to Daddy, but she acted like a nurse, first touching Daddy's neck, wrist, his feet. I didn't understand any of this, then she went to the bathroom, ran the water and returned with a wet towel. *Ma* began to wash Daddy's face and was talking really low, she was doing this in a caring way. I stood there watching, looking at the two of them. I then heard footsteps, my sister Delnora entered the room, seeing my father. The girl jumped straight up towards the ceiling. I had never seen anything like that! My brother Noddie, the same as me sat on the bed beside my father, my brother Larry, sister Tia and Irene were kept in the back, they were too young to be exposed I guess.

The whole event was getting too much for me, so I went downstairs and out to the back porch to catch some air for how long I was out there, I don't know, but I was joined by Noddie, my brother and then Delnora. Then there was some commotion as I looked into the dining room. I saw some firemen. They had a stretcher and sheets, up the stairs they went. I could hear them walking across the ceiling towards the back room, then heard them come back across the ceiling as they started down the narrow stairway. I could hear them struggling with my father's body. They had to tip the stretcher straight up towards the ceiling to turn the corner to go straight down the hallway. I got stiff thinking they were going to drop or slip my father's body. I walked back out to the back porch. I couldn't handle it. They were gone.

There seemed to be a gloom about the house. As I went to the front door standing there looking off into nothing, a black cat jumped up on the steps and acted like he wanted in. I kicked at him, scaring him off. It bothered me. I didn't know how to take it. I had too much to deal with now. As it went during those days everyone stayed at the deceased person's house until the body was buried. *Ma*, me and Aunt Corrine were showered with responses of condolences. My father's death over shadowed the fact that I was to go into the Army on the 15th of this same month of May. Daddy died on the 9th and was to be buried on the 13th. My mother in no way was going to allow this, not on the 13th was her husband going to be buried, no way. The 14th alright, but not the 15th, so the 14th ok. Now, Daddy had looked forward to me going into the Army, me getting myself straight, growing older and being a good man and I wasn't going to let him down. I was still going into the Army on the 15th, I swear! Now, the night Daddy died, I disappeared, yes I did.

Everyone was looking for me. It was decided to allow me to walk it off. But I had only gone a block away up to my buddy's house. Black Paul's house, Ms. Flowers, Paul's mother had heard of my father's passing already. She hugged and kissed me as I made my way up her stairs to her son's room. Once in the room, we sat there, talked a little and I pulled my stash out my rainy day package, taking a 20 cut. Paul and me sat and shot dope, again until we were crawling around on the floor. Once again I said, so the same routine, we were going to do. I dumped the gee (dope) into the cooker, watered it down, lit the candle. I picked the cooker up, reached it over the candle when all of a sudden something slapped the cooker out of my hand straight across the room. All the way across the room. The top hit the wall as if it was shot out of a gun. It scared the hell out of Paul and me. Damn, if it didn't make me lose my high. I mean I was dead sober, straight as a sunbeam.

We looked around the room waiting for something else to come off. I was so scared I spoke out, Hey Dad don't do this man. I'm going to get off. Do you hear me? No reply, but I was shook. My boy Paul had already opened his door and was standing in the hallway, he didn't want any of this, and he wanted me out, out of his room, out of his house. So, I took my leave, once out I walked back to the house. People were sitting, looking all sad.

People I didn't even know, all around, all over, too much. I couldn't take this Cuz. There is Cuz. When Aunt Frances, Dougie's (Cuz) mother had died, two cousins walked and walked and walked. We walked all night, morning came and we were still walking, not saying a word. The world was there, then I noticed I was alone. Cuz was not with me. Cuz was in Nam. He had been drafted months ago. I then realized how fucked up I was about my father dying.

Yes, I had walked all night long and there was a death but it was years ago. It was when Cuz's mother, my Aunt Frances had died. I had relived it in my sorrow, I cried. I found myself sitting on our steps 2675 Pennsylvania Avenue overlooking everything, nothing had changed. I just sat there and I sat there. Finally returning to the house, I climbed the stairs and slept like there was no tomorrow. The next day I awoke, cleaned up, went downstairs to join all of the folks down there. They greeted me with no questions to where I had been. After awhile a strange man came in, the funeral guy. I didn't like him, didn't know him but didn't like him. *Ma* and Aunt Corrine were seemingly at odds about something. *Ma* called me to the table and said "Obie, you have to choose a casket for Daddy babe". Who me? "Yes, what do you want for Daddy, babe?" I looked and looked, I chose this pretty bronze coffin. Yes, this one. The man said it's expensive, my mother cut him off saying my son said that one. All was well, handle it *Ma*. I thought that one Daddy had told of Veterans' funerals, how tough they were. My father was going out in grand style, top shelf, yea. The room and the house was getting brighter and a breeze could be felt coming in all of the windows, yes, it was getting easier to bare.

11th of May, time ticking away, minute by minute, hour by hour. Come on the 14th, come on. Now, I had plenty of clothes, but no suit, dress suits the kind one would wear to church that is. My buddy, Fat Robbie, yea he was square, he had some. So, I pulled Fat Robbie up, he was glad to lend me a black dress suit to wear even a nice tie to blend it out, shirt, shoes, drawers, socks, you know I had them. I'm ready. The 14th came as I knew it would. We had the funeral, it was a trip. I was ready to go to it but not ready to see my father, not as I had seen him last. I sat there on that front row (sober now) with my mind closed. I couldn't see the coffin even though it was right in front of us.

People came up, shook our hands, said what they had to say and moved on. When the family first came in, we or should I say they viewed, I just sat down on the front row, so the preacher spoke over my Dad. I don't remember if anyone sang or not, but as the funeral was to close and we were to take the last look, I stood there in total shock! I looked and looked, my father had reverted to a young man again. He was me, I was him, it was me in the coffin, a mirror image, the thin mustache, his haircut was sharp. Man, did he look good! I must have stood there for 15 minutes or more, they had to pull me away. I didn't see anyone else, hear anyone else. Into the limo to the most beautiful graveyard I had ever seen, but I didn't like the grave site but it was far, seemingly off by itself as I looked around I noticed a grave, it housed a Captain. I thought, well at least Daddy is in good company, it made things a little better.

We left Daddy to rest. The gravesite was in the City limits so I would come back to visit when I get back from Nam. I thought, I'll be back Daddy, I'll be back, I promise I thought over and over all the way home. We got to the house and my mother shrieked, that black cat was back, he was trying to get in the cellar window, once again he was scared away. No sooner did we get into the house, when the wind started to blow like crazy, paper, trash, any stuff was blowing all over the place. Then it began to rain. Man was it coming down, then thunder and lightening, the lights started to flicker, it was wild. As we looked around at one another, one of us is missing, missing? Yes, my brother Noddie, where was he? A yell from up the stairs came, up here, up here. Everyone hit the stairs. In the back room was my brother curled up in my father's bed, the mattress was indented where Daddy had laid. The room smelled like dead flowers, the boy was asleep there with it seemingly like all hell was breaking lose, the boy had ran out of the funeral home during the service because he didn't want to bury his father causing an uproar from my mother, yelling Lord you're taking my husband and my son away. But I still had to leave in the morning. I had thought I had to. I had promised I would! I was going tomorrow, so help me! I didn't do any drugs that night.

The house was clearing out now. The people were beginning to go home. Too much traffic in the house to really go to bed. My room was the middle room that led to the bathroom so for sure I wouldn't get much sleep. So, I made my way to the living room and just so happen Daddy's chair at the window was empty, great. I sat there thinking about what had come about, excluding all of the people walking about, what was going on outside.

My mind drifted to thoughts of Daddy, his smile, him walking down the street, of him and I walking around the Harbor all around Pig Town, Daddy with my sisters and brothers, even how he cried over Old Blackie, the dog dying. I could clearly see him telling me about his time overseas but what stood out in my memory was that whole week that Daddy's sight came back, yes, his sight came back, he saw again, if it was shadows or how clear it was only he could tell.

Me and Aunt Corrine along with Daddy was in the kitchen, I was frying some bacon and eggs, it was a Wednesday, yes a Wednesday because Aunt Corrine was off from work, only on Wednesdays. She was ironing some of my clothes. My father was sitting at the window near the kitchen sink. I sat down at the far top of the table, ready to throw down on these eggs and bacon, when my father turned from the window and looked my way. He didn't flinch, saying boy what have you done to your hair, you need a haircut, son. My aunt dropped the iron to the floor. I sat there with food in my mouth. He stood up with tears in his eyes. "Obie you can see, oh my God! Thank you, thank you Jesus!" My aunt was running all round the small kitchen. Still sitting in the chair, my father took steps towards me. I didn't know if to do a break for the back door or not. As usual, I was wasted, but I stayed still.

Daddy reached out, pulled me in and ran his fingers through my nappy bush, saying "What's this?" "A bush". "A what boy?" "A bush Dad, a bush." I felt good, I had one of those inside smiles going on. Man, I may never feel that way again as I did at that moment. He went to the back porch, sunny, it was a very nice weather day, he just stood there, then to the front door. He asked me to go get the kids and "How is Dee (my mother)?" I replied "Fine." I slid pass him and embarked up to *Ma*'s to get my sisters and brothers. I told *Ma* about his sight coming back. She whooped, cried and praised God, but didn't volunteer to go down to the house, so I left it alone, gathered up my brothers and sisters and away we went. Man, it was great! Really great, a lot of hugging and laughing. Aunt Corrine cooked, we ate and laughed some more.

Soon our smiles were to be turned upside down because on May 7th Daddy was blind as a bat again, two days before he died (wild huh?) Really wild. I think about it often now. But we took it that God gave him sight, then took him away, for God is good. God is good always. A lot of things formulated in my mind as I set in that chair. I was interrupted from my thoughts by noise outside, but as I opened my eyes, it seemed like I was high like I had smoked some real good Herb.

Everything was extra clear, sharp, and bright, it seemed that I was looking in, that there was this movie going on and I was watching everything going on. An outsider, not really part of the activity, but still a part of it. I began to talk to myself in my mind. I did this every time I ran into some killer junk to get control of the high, to settle my thoughts down to level off the effect of the drugs, but this was different.

I didn't know what this was, I thought may be I was having a flash back to some of that acid I had taken at one time. I took three tablets of purple haze once and I tripped for three, four days. I took them in the pool room one Saturday night, I then got hungry for some chocolate cake, so I went down to the ice cream shop where Cuz's girl worked, got a piece of cake and jumped up on this wall and sat there eating. I got relaxed there. I must had set an hour and a half or so when I felt my skin crawl, then a pulling sensation, then I saw me jump out of me (yea). I jumped out of myself, out of my body! I sat there looking at me looking back at me! Then I started to walk away from myself. I sat there wide-eyed, couldn't move as I saw myself look back at me, then turned the corner.

I don't know how long I sat there facing in the direction of the corner, but I do know Stella Brown, Cuz's girl called out to me, "See you Obie" as she was going home after the ice cream shop had closed. Don't ask what happened next, but I do remember it started to rain. I was so messed up I could see the raindrops, each one of them, I saw the blue color in the water. I saw the little window box inside each raindrop. I saw them hit the ground, the explosion and water volcano and water lave spilling out of the funnel at the top of the volcano. I saw the paths the rain was falling from the sky. I saw the opening spaces and I tried to walk in between the raindrops. Man, I was out of it! Gone. Well, I was soaking wet and fucked up. I made it back to the poolroom, only a half block down the street.

Now, this pool room named Frank's had a steep stairway straight up, with 21 steps, no landing midway, just up, up, up or that's how it felt that night. Those steps seemed to never want to end. Well, I made it, the top I made it to the window bench, almost where I had smoked that good herb at one time in the past. I sat there spaced out! There was some ugly niggers in the joint, man I mean ugly! Asshole ugly. They had to scare the shit out of their mothers when the doctor placed them on their mother's chest that first time I thought as I sat there.

I got tickled, tickled pink the more I looked at them, the more I laughed. I got loud and started to point at people. They were really fucked, some were short, some were big and funny built. Why don't he take a shave, fix himself up or something, I thought, but I was saying this stuff out loud. The guys thought I was fucking with them (just cracking) making fun and they were laughing with me. I was on a roll, no harm was taken.

Nobody got mad or angry because very seldom did I get off like that. Man, I was tore up. I laughed until I had tears coming out of my eyes and my stomach hurt. My boy black Paul came in, he enjoyed me carrying on, then I told him about the acid and he decided to stay with me, because he told me he had heard of people having bad trips awhile on this stuff, especially if something bad came off and he stayed close the entire time I was off on that acid. This memory crossed my mind as I sat there trying to figure out what was going on with me now.

Had the death of my father driven me crazy, had the drugs come back to haunt me? Was my mind trying to play tricks on me or was I just coming down, jonesing (yea) I must be jonesing? But still Nam was waiting in the wings.

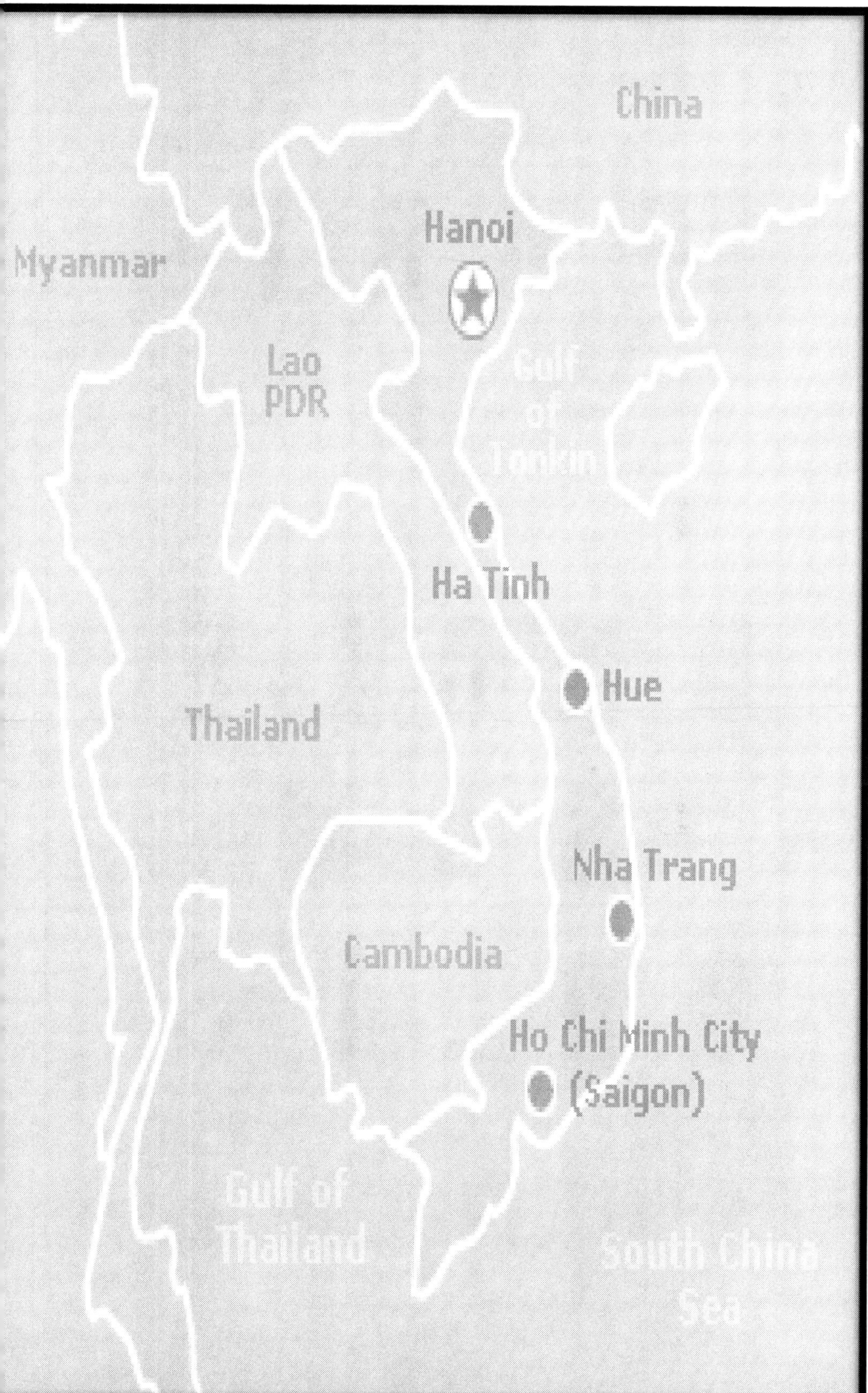
China
Hanoi
Myanmar
Lao
PDR
Gulf
of
Tonkin
Ha Tinh
Hue
Thailand
Nha Trang
Cambodia
Ho Chi Minh City
(Saigon)
Gulf of
Thailand
South China
Sea

PART II

UNCLE SAM CALLS

Chapter 5
Uncle Sam calls

That night I didn't sleep. If I did, I don't know, but daylight hit, I gathered myself up, took a *Clark Kent* (wash up) ready to go. Aunt Corrine's door opened, she had stayed home today. She went downstairs. I heard pots rattling, then smelled bacon cooking. She made Cream of Wheat, bacon, eggs and toast and jelly with chocolate milk on the side (decent)! Little was said. I looked up at the clock, 9:00 a.m. was coming at me.

Aunt Corrine disappeared, came back opened her hand, $20.00 she had in it. I smiled saying save that for stamps so you can write me back, ok. She smiled and hugged me tightly. The poor woman didn't know I had $1,000.00 stuffed in my socks and damn near 150 bags of heroin taped to my chest and six sets of guns (needles) taped to my thigh. I was ready, alright, all was right with me.

Time passed, the black car pulled in front of the house, my boy Aaron the karate fighter (and he sold herb down the way) said he would pick me up and take me downtown to the reception center on Water Street and Pratt. On time he was and away we went. We talked about money, girls and lock ups on the drive to downtown. As we neared the place, Aaron lit up a joint, we hit the joint, he always had a good blend. Here it is, Aaron said. We looked at one another all high and broke out laughing, shook hands and parted.

Inside I went, two soldiers stood at the front door. I peeped over at them, then opened the door. Man all kind of activity was going on. Men all over the place, this was a zoo, noise up the hiney, soldiers were howling orders, pushing people all about. I checked in at this table. The man asked for my registration card. I had forgotten I said I would go back home and get it and come back (bullshit). If I had gotten out of there (go back where) my ass! But the soldier directed me to a room. I had a replacement card in nothing flat.

The men and myself were shuffled room to room for hours. Lunchtime was coming up (good). I could find me a bathroom and get off I thought (no). They had us group together and marched us down a hallway down some stairs to a big yard right in the middle of the building outside. I tell you man, my plans to get off were shot to hell! I'm disgusted, mad and ready to blow this spot, but these soldiers are acting like jailhouse guards (for real). They are MP soldiers and act serious about their jobs.

A door opens and more soldiers come out the door with pallets of white boxes, millions of these white boxes, there are more pallets with soft drinks and packaged cakes. These box lunches and drinks and cake hit the spot. But I wanted to get off! I had to find a way to do what I wanted to do. After eating, we went back inside the building. I'm looking into offices as we pass them. I'm looking for a coffee cup. Coffee areas, I need a spoon, a steel spoon. I have everything else. Ain't no wine bottle around here to use.

I'm on the hunt, dead serious about getting off. There's one over there where that woman is, but it's behind the counter, how to get it? How to get back there? Oh, ok she calls me back to sign papers, ok. I will cop the spoon when I am called back there, like a hawk I watched her every move she made. Time passed, I waited, then I heard my name called. Ok, but it was a dude, a dude called me not the lady I had been counting on to call me. I was insulted! I sat at his desk mad as hell. When he finished with me, I had this great idea, the floor plan was laid out, so on my way out. I took the scenic route. I tried to cover the complete area, looking on every desk along the way. I needed a spoon, a steel one. Hey there! There it was, unguarded, all alone.

As I walked pass the spoon disappeared from the desk. I palmed it in my hand, it was safely kept. I was going to take care of it. I was going to watch over it (I swore), out the swinging gate I went, one happy camper. Now, I have to find somewhere to get off. This was my main focus now, the hell with the rest of this shit going on. Now, I knew they had to have a shit house somewhere in this place and they did. I un-taped my chest and thigh, got my outfit together and hit up.

Now it was on (ok) I set on the floor up against the wall watching the happenings. The old man that seemed to be giving me a lot of directions interested me so I watched him, he had a lot of people running up to him but he had civilian clothes on, he was no soldier but he was somebody. I sat there for a long time, then the soldier rounded us up once more. They started calling names, they lined up and disappeared out of an open door. I was called, I lined up, and walked out of the door, there a bus awaited us. We climbed aboard and sat down.

We were driven to Fort Holabird Reception Center down in Dundalk in Baltimore County. The Army gave you a physical, tested you for brain power, and classified each person to the dream list of what they wanted you to do in the Army. Yea, now a lot of the guys didn't want to go into the Army, Navy, Marines, Air Force, nothing and their option to say so was coming up soon. See, we had not taken the oath yet. The oath to America the beautiful. America, my home sweet home from sea to shining sea. Yea, I thought for I had seen the purple mountains and all that stuff as fucked up as I could get, I was sure I had seen it all. I thought no doubt! Anyway, this place was where you really joined up for the services to protect America. Now, I saw a lot of guys with Army clothes on so I began to listen around. I overheard they would take our civilian clothes and give us Army greens. They were going to cut our hair, but these guys had hair, so they must had been through this already. They were already real soldiers, some of them even had stripes on their sleeves. Well, I had to strip, so I had to clean up a little and I was going to need a stash spot for my hardware.

It was time to make a friend, an Army friend, one that knew his way around, one who knew the ropes, or may be needed a little cash and I was loaded with cash (you know) so I met this young private first class from Dundalk, blonde-headed kid. For a white boy he came off wild, he was not a soldier by a long shot, a young head was what he was, a hippie wanna be. He walked around singing rock songs, carefree as hell. Well, I just knew he would go for a joint.

I made major plans on making him a contact person. I needed a mule, a stash person who was on this post. These people were going to strip and search us for drugs and anything else we were not to have on or with us. The young black soldier, a first class private also was hard to read. I didn't want to go at him and get turned in by my own kind, he might be straight or one of those niggers that had found a home in this man's Army.

I had to walk a chalk line with him. But as a last resort, I knew money could change you. If need be, I would hit him up with some ends (money) (yea, that will work). I thought back to Blondy, after chow (that was what they called eating food, breakfast, lunch, dinner). Blondy would disappear and believe me, I was looking out for him. He and two other white boys seemed to be tight. May be he was off with them.

Now, after chow, we were free for the day. We haven't gotten our hair cut, or got our greens yet, nor had anyone treated us as soldiers. No formation, saluting, stuff like that and thank God they had not searched us yet! Not to mention a physical exam, me with all of these tracks on my body (Man).

Blondy and the other soldier stayed in a building next to ours. Man, I started to sniff in the air, hoping to smell herb, no luck, just white boy music. After being on point for a couple of days. Hello, Herb! I knew that smell, oh boy! I'm in the game now! I broke out of the door, nose high, sniffing the vapors, tracking vapors to its source, down the side of the building around the back. There it is! Yeah! Old Blondy and four, yes four of his boys, throwing down big time! I approached on the low, stood there, didn't say a thing, just stood there just like any other good head.

The joint was passed to me, little ole me, not even a soldier yet, in the mix. Well, one good turn deserves another. When it was down to a roach, I pulled out my shit or should I say Aaron's shit. Anyhow, one of the dudes took the joint, sniffed it and flamed on, he pulled and pulled again, gagged but held on, breathed and went for seconds. He then gave up, choking and choking, then in between coughing he said Man, this is alright. Everybody smiled. His buddy had to reach over and grab the joint out of his hand, he hit, his buddy hit, we all hit. The party was on. Yea, and I was in (Old Blackie in the mix) without saying Blondy was in charge of the group, I was in.

Blondy and me got tight, three days at this post with four days to go. The search was due to fall any minute, damn near all of the test and personnel stuff is out of the way. Search, haircut, Army greens, then oath of a legion, then off to New Jersey Boot Camp. That's what Blondy tells me. Now, always on the job drunk, sober, high or indifferent, us soldiers were having our tea party.

I was looking around, I notice the building, it was three stories, three big windows across on all three levels, then the back had a fire escape with stairs to the ground level to the ground. The building also had a lattice type screen storage area cut into the bottom of this building. Just perfect. Perfect to stash my products out of sight out of mind, and to think I didn't even have to use Blondy and the boys. Yeah, I liked this plan. So be it! Well, you know what I did. I stashed my shit there, a lot of pressure off of me now, let's play Army. Notice I said play!

Breakfast that morning, eggs, bacon, shit on a shingle, fried potatoes, biscuits, grits, French toast, a hell of a spread, plus white or chocolate milk, Coke, Sprite, Pepsi soda to boot. The Army really threw down and it's free! After chow, this big, really huge white guy, starched down, boots looking like a mirror, face looked hard as stone, yelled, "Get your dumb asses lined up by twos". You couldn't but do what he said do. We lined up. Ready, march! March, I thought so, I just picked my feet high off the ground and let it fall back down, picking the other up, then down. Then he yelled your left. I was on the wrong foot, so I made the adjustment and marched on, and on, down the walkway to a cross lane on down to a building to the right.

The sign said "Barber". Now, I had been growing this hair, this bush hairstyle for two whole years (you now what I mean) two whole years. Now I had heard they were going to chop it all off, just zip-zip, no style to it! Doom ran through my mind, no way. But I'm locked in, drafted, a prisoner of the Army and I hadn't even really joined up yet! Damn! But I can show my ass still. I'll show them. I don't give a damn. So my turn came for a haircut, yes, but my way. I told the old man to give me a "Yul Brenner", cut it all off, then shave it crystal ball clean! And he did just that (man, my head looked like a number seven pool ball). The man even spread some grease on it, it was sharp! I jumped the door, the Sergeant saw me and yelled "Look, a real piece of shit". "We have a real asshole here, do we." Then, right then and there I knew the war was on!

The other Sergeant was looking at me like they were taking notes as I walked past, shit if I cared. Fuck them. I lined back up, one of the Sergeants came off asking me where I came from? Here, I said, here where, he questioned. "Back here," I replied, not here! He replied, "We don't have brown shit around here asshole! "Here, where?" "Baltimore! I yelled back" *I can do this yelling thing too* I thought. Baltimore huh? "Yea, Baltimore City, here!" Sergeant said, "Well this ain't Baltimore boy, this is the county boy! My county! And you don't act or look like an asshole in my county! So go with your dumb ass and pick up every piece of hair that you had cut off and bring it back here to me." Shit, if I thought, this nigger is cold crazy. And I stood there ready to rumble! Another Sergeant came up on my right, then my left. The Sergeant stood there as if he was waiting for me to move.

Now, I had been *banked* (jumped by more than one man) before, I can't win this! But I can't jack either so I just stood my ground! The three of them yelled, talked about my mother, Baltimore City, like a dog! I took it all, but didn't say a word. As the other guys got their hair cut, we waited, almost dinner time and we were still waiting then (line up troops was yelled), we lined up, one of the Sergeants walked over, stopped aside me, told me to get out of the line, I did.

Another Sergeant yelled forward, march. The line began to move forwards, man by man passed me and the standing Sergeant at the end of the line was nearing, then the end. The Sergeant said this is your place, get to the line, march, hup two! Man the handwriting was on the wall, now for sure! Man, there must had been at least 500 men or more in our section, all had to be fed and I was the last to eat! I had to wolf the food down!

The Sergeants were pressing me, they even sat at the empty table I had sat at staring at me as I ate, drinking coffee and making little cracks about Baltimore City and my baldhead. Being through enough, it didn't phase me. We played this game as a little boy, but we talked about one another's mother. We call it *"motherology"* and these fools were amateurs, but to crack bad would only piss them off! They hassled me all the way until I left Ft. Holabird.

Well, we had expected to ship out and now it was staring us in the face, everyone was rushing to get their stuff together. The only stuff I was worried about was under our porch stashed away safely, but once again I had to be on guard about a search and there wasn't anywhere private to tape my stash onto my body, but I had to find a way.

Now, I had seen an empty barrack two buildings over from our barracks but I had not checked it out during my stay here so I found time to check it out fast. The door had a lock on it and all of the windows were shut, but like ours it had that back porch, but it had a straight door wooden panel running clear across the entire back. That was on time, that is where I would do the taping out of sight (yes). Sarge had told us 1900 hours we were moving out that was after dinner (chow) so I was ready, plans were in order. Just follow through. Well, I did. We boarded the bus and rode and rode, so four and half hours later, New Jersey and this post called Fort Dix.

Fort Dix? I don't know nothing about a Fort Dix. The place was big, we must have drove across it for 18- 20 minutes and we were still going. Finally, we stopped, dark as hell out on a big lot. Then the lights went on and a whole lot of hollering and screaming. These soldiers with Smokey the bear hat on, pushing, kicking at people, cussing at the top of their lungs. These were drill sergeants. They rounded us up, had us throw our bag on the ground in front of ourselves, standing at attention next to the piles. Some young soldiers were digging through our stuff, but they didn't search us. I sure was glad about this (home free). We gathered our stuff, they called us in alphabetical order as to what barracks we were to sleep in. For the first time I realized how long it took to get to the letter (W), it's way down the road if you wait to hear it, for the first time I heard the word platoon.

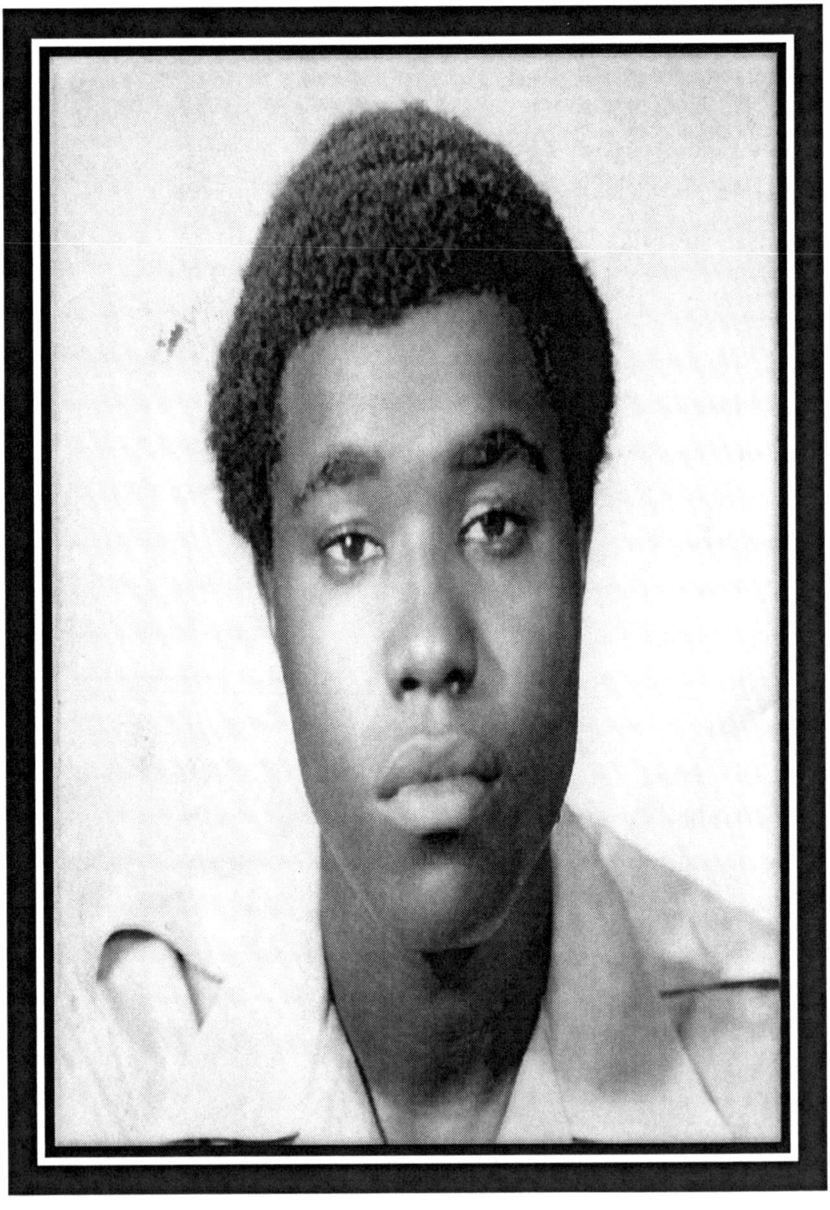

Chapter 6
Basic Training

My platoon was the fifth (5th) Platoon, with a company of 200 men to do basic training as one, the Sergeant said but as I looked around, all I saw was a bunch of Blacks all from either Philly, New York, New Jersey and me the only one from B-More of damn near 200 men. This looked like they had cleaned out the ghettos of all of these major cities. There was a field first, an E-7 in charge of the company and an E-6 Sergeant that had 2 tours in Nam, he was from Alabama. Two more E-sixes from Georgia and one white E-6 built like a tank. He boasted how he had maxed the entire non-commission officer school and could do 250 pushups. That was impressive, a 250 count, but it took me to thinking of all of this pepper and no salt, looked like no white boys had been called up in the draft, but on second thought I liked the make up for I saw future customers for my product.

Now, I noticed also that I was getting over again and again. I still had my stash and I had not been shook down, so I started to getting off. Now the bathroom toilet stalls were open, but if I got up early I could slide into the head (toilet) cook up, get off and coast through the morning. I would make up enough junk to carry me over through lunchtime. This went on for four straight weeks. I ran, did push ups, did the ladder exercises, marched like the rest of the guys, all the while high. No one seemed to catch on to all of the energy I had, but the Sergeant thought I had a mood change problem, some times I was hostile and bossy because I would get disgusted at some of the guys that just seemed to quit at certain tasks, until one day a guy from one of the other platoons in my same company came up and told me to give the other guys the blues. He shocked me right off, because he said "You dumb MF don't you think no one out here know you are fucked up all the time man". You're gonna fuck around and bust your heart with that shit and all of this exercising." Now, I had seen this boy doing push ups as punishment for doing something wrong from time to time. He would throw down with the muscle bound Sergeant and do push ups until he couldn't lift his body off the ground anymore. He would fly through the ladder rope to eat lunch and dinner after the Sergeants would grease the bars to make holding your grip on the bars hard. This chump was a brick house, tight, he could have played football or something, but most of all he was down with me. He had been down with what made me tick. Now, I wondered who else was for all of the guys had come from major cities. They had to know the signs of a head, now up until the 5th week I had not sold any junk to anyone.

We drilled, marched, and trained minute to minute, but we were to have a break. The rifle range training was the second part of our training and we could mingle more than we had before. The entire company would be on the range together and we had room to roam around while waiting to shoot targets. It was loose. Shortly after starting range shooting, a brother came up from out of nowhere, he sat down beside me. We talked about those little birds that were all over the rifle range walking around with no fear of the rifle fire and all of the noise going on. I replied "I guess they are use to it." Then he changed the subject.

"Man, where can I get some of that high material you have been getting huh?" I just looked at him, thinking, is this a set up or what. I had learned that in each class that went through basic training, the Army had men that were CID agents that were undercover agents that posed as GIs and would lock your ass up and send you to Leavenworth jail forever and if drugs, or stealing in the Army, they would bury you deep in the belly of the jail. So, being on point, I had to handle this with a long handle spoon. So, I came off with "The doctor gives me medicine for my nerves and migraines I suffer from." "They carry side effects, you know?" He looked at me steadily, then shook his head, but said "Man you sure look like you be feeling it." "You want to sell a couple of them pills?" I stated, "I don't know man". I don't know how they will effect anybody else. We were feeling one another out.

    I was waiting for more background from him, but he was called by one of the boys. He stood saying, I'm in Bravo Company, 2nd Platoon. I didn't need his name, because it was on his suit's name tag. I put it to memory, now if he was looking for downers, I didn't have any but I had the mother of downers, heroin, but I had to check this dude out further. Now, we had put enough time into basic training that we were free to go the Post Exchange (PX), barber shop and visit other companies anywhere in the basic training area but no further that was off limits. So, I strolled over to Bravo Company, 2nd Platoon.

    I entered the building up to the second floor. When I opened the door to the 2nd Platoon, every head in there turned to face me. A stranger, I stood there, scanned the huge bay looking for expectant customers, didn't see him, so I slow walked down the center hall. Now only the Sergeants walked the center aisle in the bays, so who in the hell was this? Midway I saw my man laying on his rack (bed). I kicked his footlocker, he raised, smiles, rolled out of the rack. He offered me a seat on the footlocker and he made me comfortable. He told his mates that we were cousins, cousins really I thought. Cousins and I was checking him out to be the police or CID, an Army snitch or something. Him and I talked and talked, no talk about pills, drugs of any kind. He even allowed me to see family pictures he had a phat sister back home, but I kept that to myself. Now, I had a small sample of heroin as a tester (a try outer). As I stood up to leave, as we shook hands, I palmed the plastic package to him and said this should do you and may be a friend, snort it now and walk this time down the side aisle of the room. The next day came, just as the one before that had, up, ate, ran, back to the company, lunch, off to the rifle range, same as before. My man came over, he asked for five of the same packages he had received as a sample but this time he was ready to buy some. Well, hello again, I replied. I sold my stuff as six packs, twelve ½ packs and 25 pack bundles at $3.00 a piece, he liked the deal and said a 6 pack (of cost). I agreed, now remember we are into our 6th week of basic training, all that's left is rifle shooting and awards and obstacle course exam, then completion and graduation.

The full 12 weeks training, yes not 8 weeks but 12 weeks. We were to be infantry soldiers, then to 12 weeks of advance infantry training at another post somewhere with an offering the Sergeant had said for a few of the best of the cycle. I didn't know what that meant but he had said that a few of the best. Anyhow, I said the 6 pack and don't you know more orders started to come in. I told my man I would only fill his orders, nobody else and for every two 6 packs he would get a free bag for himself. We had it going on.

Soon, I had not only my Company, but three of the Companies in our square parade grounds rocking. Money was coming in like crazy, like I had taken this little guy who bunked over top of my head, in the top bunk where I slept I called Little Camden, he was from Camden, NJ. He was only about 5' tall, I often thought how he had gotten into this man's army. He had not finished high school, not even junior high school. He could barely read. I wrote all of his letters to home for him. He couldn't even jump up to reach the ladder bar and hand over hand to earn the right to eat meals as each man had to do daily, 3 times a day just to eat (exercise) really, he couldn't finish any of the 3 miles and no way the 5 mile runs back to the Company to earn the right to leave the Company area. He was one of the guys I use to give hell to, but he was alright once you got to know him. He loved the service, it was the best thing that had ever happened to him, being drafted, free meals, a bed, clothes and $60.00 a month pay. He would count his $60.00 over and over and over. I had told him to pin the cash to his drawers for safety cause we had creepers in our Platoon room and Little Camden ate like he was always starving. He begged everybody for what they didn't eat. He would scope around the tables for leftovers and ask for them and chow down. If you didn't like something, we would get it anyway because we knew Little Camden would be coming to clean our pates.

The entire Platoon fed this little man (I lie not) and he didn't gain any weight. Well, without my knowledge Little Camden had also developed a little yearn, a need to be accepted by others in the bay. He had tried some heroin. Now his mind wasn't ready for drugs, he just didn't have the mentality for this! How he even thought to get into this, I don't know. Now, our Company was 2nd in status for field, track and physical training. First place belonged to big black the guy who had pulled me up for bitching at the weaker guys. Only because of big black really did his company carry first place status because of him. He could do it all, letter for letter. But even his company was falling off in their tasks.

The Sergeants, I had heard thought there was a URI going on or something (Upper Respiratory Infection) but it was heroin, heroin pulling the men's performance down. Sooner or later, it was gonna come out what was going on I thought. So, I decided to pull back a little. I decided to sell only every other day. The effects didn't hit for a few days, then all hell seemed to break lose. Man, the men were goofing, they were throwing up, going to sick call, getting mean with my man and to top it off, Little Camden cracked wide open in the mess hall at lunch time for me to give him some junk to take off the edges, cause he was ill. Well, for those that didn't know, they damn sure did now. I had to get my shit together fast. I could feel the cell shutting at Leavenworth, this fool had dry snitched on me!

Man, I had thousands of dollars in my foot locker, drugs in my shaving kit, drugs in socks, in suit pockets, right in the open that had laid safely kept and this fool had put me in harms way. I know the Sergeants had to hear what that damn fool had said, but I sat there thinking what now? My mind was racing, I had to put a plan together fast! Straight after chow, just as usual we went back to the bay, got our rifles, bullet pouches, helmet and liners and then 15 minutes later formation. Then we would leave for the range, not today for me! No way! We returned to the bay. I started cleaning up shop!

Cleared up my stuff, the cash and headed for off Post, walking down the road, that road seemed to never end. I started to trot, in good shape (thanks to the Army training, I got a second wind and onwards I trotted). I slowed down as I heard a truck coming up to my rear. I just knew it was the MPs coming for me! Then, "Hey man, you need a ride (huh?)" a young PFC (private first class) RA (regular Army) (enlisted man). "Yea! Whew!" I jumped up into the 5 ton truck, down the road to the gate and out. Now the PFC was not going downtown but $20.00 changed his mind and direction and downtown we went. I was looking for any bank or western union office (then there she blows, a bank!) "Stop, stop, I yelled." Thank you man and I almost ran into the door of the bank.

It was still open with 10 minutes to spare, 12:50 p.m. or may be 12:51 p.m. Anyway I sat at the desk to open up an account. No problem $5,000.00 passbook account. I was alley-alley in free! I even opened up a safe deposit box. The woman who signed had no questions about what I was doing, but I had all of these drugs in this shaving kit pouch. What the hell, I thought I'd buy another one. I put the pouch in the long slender box, gave the lady a smile as I left the bank. Now, to get back to the Post.

Well, $20.00 can move mountains and it did. I rode back in a new Buick Century, 4 door sedan, out at the gate, walked in and stopped by the MP at the gate $20.00 again and I walked up the road. Now, I knew I was busted, but not for no drugs, not for any cash stashed, just rumors, just talk. I had to think about an excuse, ahhh, I had one! I would tell them I was going AWOL because of my girl. I had called home and was told she was messing around on me with a chump that I hated and I was going to kill the both of them, but a PFC had picked me up and talked some sense into me. It or she wasn't worth it. Yea, as I got closer to the training area, I got kind of shaky.

The Company area was empty, not a soul in sight. I decided on what to do. I thought I'm going to the range so that's what I did. I went into the Barracks, got my gear and started to walk towards the range, walking changed into trotting, then I started to chant to myself. "I'm going to be an airborne soldier. I'm going to live a life of danger. I'm going to be in Viet Nam" over and over and over I chanted the verse. This song was taking it's toll, something was going on, my feet kept on moving, my breath was steady. I was in the groove, 1 mile, 2 miles, 3 miles, steady singing louder and louder. I added the second verse, "You can make it! Gotta make it! I'm going to be an airborne soldier. I'm going to face a life of danger, I'm going to fight in Viet Nam", loud and moving down the road I went.

I saw a car coming toward me about ½ miles ahead but the road being straight and flat, you could see for miles to the skyline ahead. The car got nearer and nearer, finally right close to me still running. There a MP and field first sat in the front seats. They didn't stop, they pulled behind me, following behind me. I peeped back, Sarge was smoking, the MP looked serious as a heart attack. I kept on singing and trotting, not missing a step. I sang louder as I got tired, a second, third, and fourth wind. I was running like a real track star, booking, the sign said Range #9 with the arrow pointing to the left as I bared left, a voice behind me yelled Range #12, ahh man, another mile and a piece, my heart sank! Gotta make it! Gotta make it! I pulled on everything that was in me to make it, the Jeep stayed back there all the way to Range #12.

I made it, my lungs burned, my legs felt like they were going to fall off, my feet, my poor feet were extra heavy. Finally, I stopped completely. Sarge told me to walk it off! I walked up and down the external of the range (gun lane), then I walked towards the gun lane, found the alphabet W, took my place, got on line, shot 50 meters, 100 meters, 500 meters, 750 meters, 1000 meters. Surprise to me, I was tearing the targets up, knocking them down again and again and at the 1000 meter targets I was sharp! Man, and I was sober, cold sober!

When the Gunnery Marine Sergeant, who ran the ranges, tapped me on my helmet and said, "Damn good son, damn good!" I felt like an airborne soldier for real! As I walked back to zero ground (safety zone on the range) a PFC came over and pointed in the direction of a clump of sergeants. Man! I'm dead, I thought all of these sergeants in one place. I slow walked over there, saluted. There was also a captain. "Walker, where in the hell have you been son?" Field First asked. I started to spin my tale (tell my story), upon finishing they looked at one another, it was so quiet, I could hear the wind blowing and this was a still day. They just looked at one another, one of the other sergeants, asked "Where do you come from son?" "Baltimore," I replied. "Baltimore, huh? How many more from Baltimore can lie like you son?" "Lie Sarge, about what?" I replied. Your girl fucked you over, you go AWOL, then have a change of heart, then run back 7 ½ miles to your true love, the Army is that right son?" "Yes Sarge, that's what I did, you said 7 ½ miles I ran," "Yes son, you ran a 4 minute mile, did you know that son?" "No Sarge". "Did you know the Army was going to classify you as a deserter son?" "Deserter, I didn't desert and where Sarge?" "I didn't even leave Fort Dix, Sarge." "Son, did you pass through the gates, did you leave the training ground son?" "Yes, Sarge". "Well, son don't you know we have a war going on son?" "Yes, Sarge, but I ain't did no deserting anywhere Sarge". "Where is your company son?" "Right over there Sarge." "Did you leave with the troops for the range with your company son?" "No, Sarge." "Did you have permission not to leave the company for this range from your Field First, son." "No Sarge". "Well, son during war times, this event could be considered AWOL and desertion son!" "Son, do you think you are a good soldier?" "Do you know or have you heard or read the Military Code of Justice son?" "Only parts of it Sarge." "Why only parts of it son?" "I didn't plan on getting into any trouble Sarge." "Well son you are in trouble!" "Do you realize that son?" "I hear you Sarge." "You hear me son, but you don't know it son?" "Yes Sarge! "Well at least you aren't completely dumb." "Have you ever killed a man son?" "No Sarge." "Would you kill a man, son?" "If he was going to kill me Sarge." "Can you shoot son?" "I guess I can Sarge." "How did you do today son?" "Did you qualify son?" "I don't know Sarge."

Finally he paused, and he motioned for the PFC to go get the shot record for today's shoot. The PFC came back, handed the papers over to the Sergeant, he then passed them to my Field First, he handed them to another Sergeant. The papers got passed around to all of the Sergeants, then to the Captain who has stood there all of the time not saying a word (not one word) did he mumble. "Son, do you know what you scored son?" "No Sarge." "Well, son you scored expert on the M-16, 4 cal, M-60 machine gun and son only thing left for you to do is the night firing son." "I don't believe an asshole like you, a cut and run cause Jessy got your girl and gone, can shoot like that! You are gonna get military justice son! Son, the Army is going to send your dumb ass to Viet Nam and as you were singing you may just luck up and fool the Airborne Division into letting your dumb ass train for the Airborne Unit, you dumb asshole. But for now son, pick up your weapon and follow this here MP back to your barracks. Do you hear me son? Son, do you hear me?" "Yes, Sergeant," I yelled.

As I was told I headed for the jeep and the MP that had gotten aboard. He started up the jeep and started to drive away. I yelled, "Hey, he hollered back, you get back to the barracks the same way you got here." And yelled "I wanna be an airborne soldier, I wanna go to Viet Nam, I wanna live a life of danger, airborne one two, one two three four" and I followed through over and over and over. This trip back to the barracks was three times further it seemed.

Upon getting back, chow was being served not only was I tired, I was hungry. I did the ladder rope, the low crawl belly slide and 25 push ups as everyone else had to do to eat at this point. Ready to go into the mess hall this PFC that was sitting on the front porch and was looking on, pulled me up at the front doorstep "You are last to eat Private, to the side with your ass, move!" I did, but as I was standing to the side and First Sergeant came out of the door, he looked at me, turned towards me and said, "Take up guard at the can there, the trash can sitting there, that big nasty green trash can, flies blowing all around, smelly, nasty trash can. I had guarded a can. Now, I did that night and every night to follow until the morning of graduation. My cash was in the bank, my stash was safe.

The Company was on the chill, that mean ole upper respiratory infection has seemed to pass. All was well for the 5th Platoon Alpha Company. But graduation night belonged to me, for that morning I didn't have to guard that dumb trash can. I skipped breakfast chow, dressed for the day. I slid back downtown to that bank, got my cash and my stash and opened shop. When the Star Spangled Banner was played, I guarantee you damn near 90% of U.S. (GIs) was heroin down. My treat because no one except dumb ass Lil Camden had blown a tip on me.

As we got to the end of the ceremony Field First had ordered a PFC to fetch me. I entered the office as a soldier, my heels locked, arms at my side, eyes straight ahead. For a minute I felt like a real Army man, a solider, fit, proud and ready to do the do overseas, come what may!

Then Field First Murphy stood, he walked around me looking me up and down, he seemed to cover my entire body even to look into my ears. I stood fast! He spoke, "Son, you made it through here, by the skin of your teeth, you violated most if not all standards of Military Code of Justice. You have made a mockery of this U.S. Army. You think you fooled anybody here at Ft. Dix, son?" "The drugs, the running off, the running back to cover your ass, son we have seen all types of young men go through here and you are a little bit brighter than most but that shit is gonna kill you son. You will end up in Nam where you will run into tons of shit! You are going to have an enemy that is going to want to kill you, that shit is waiting to kill you. You don't even know that you are trying to kill yourself, son! And damn it son, don't you realize they are sending you off to get killed."

That last statement knocked me to my knees. I thought they are sending me off to Nam to get killed, killed! This came from a man I admired, this man had years of service behind him, he had overseas bars, Korea, Okinawa, Germany, Philippines, Nam, Guam and ribbons running up his sleeves forever plus he had that long rifle with blue arm band and an Airborne insignia (man) he was laid out. This man was talking to me like a father. I remember a father, my father but I know now I had blocked his death out of my thoughts. But I locked in my mind what Field First had said about they were sending me, me and all of these other ghetto boys to die overseas.

Now, I was told my great, great grandfather was Haitian, he had come from Haiti to South Carolina, a geechee man, tall, double black, pearly white teeth, proud and fathered 14 kids and our people had never surrendered to anybody, any country warred against anybody that tried to enslave his people and had hung Napoleon's first cousin trying to enslave his people, and stayed off the U.S. Marines when the USA tried to take over his country. They went up into the mountains, and stayed there, fought off all of their oppressors, even went to eating one another when the Marines tried to starve them out and do our people proud. Now, I damn sure wasn't going to be tricked into getting killed in a war I didn't know anything about, nor was I going to get killed overseas. Everybody knew spirits can't travel overseas, damn my soul would be lost forever, no way! And I wasn't nowhere near 45 years old. Shit, I had to live to retire and live the good life. Dying would mess up all my plans. Field First had finished talking to me. I had new insight of this Viet Nam war and a lot to think about on the long ride back home to B-more and my family. Plus, I had to re-up on some product (drugs),12 weeks down in Alabama and I know they don't have any dope down there and once again I'd have to adjust, blend in and work out on the side, get a plan together to handle Viet Nam.

Now, believe me I had plenty of time to plan, that bus I caught from Ft. Dix was called a local, it stopped every 3 miles it seemed, it delivered papers, milk, stopped to pick people up from the road out of nowhere. I saw cows, barns, corn, tomatoes, wheat, soybeans, all kinds of stuff on this ride on the scenic route. When I saw the sign say York, PA I was so happy, down 83 to Baltimore, my Baltimore, my hometown! My homecoming was all the talk of the family. For the next 29 days I only stayed at

2618 Woodbrook two nights. I now know I still wasn't settled to admit my father had died and I was higher than a Georgia pine from the minute I hit town until the minute I left town. I had to find the best product I could find during my 29 day stay, that was my focus, only that. The morning I was to leave, I went pass my mother's, said goodbye to the kids, then down to 2618 to say goodbye to my aunt. She cried and asked me to send some money home to help her out. My aunt didn't say a thing about my mother and the children as if they didn't need money sent also. It bothered me, because I had heard the story about how my father and my uncle had sent my aunt money home and she fucked it up. They came home to find nothing, no money, only an excuse. This event I had to file away in my memory bank.

    At this time, I am off to Friendship National Airport of Baltimore and down to Georgia, then to Redstone Arsenal (what?). This place was for missiles, bombs, tanks and demolition depot and training. What did this have to do with being an Airborne soldier? I was told first a soldier (grunt) foot soldier, then a job and training then if accepted, specialized training like Airborne - Paratrooper training, if you are good enough. Well, I would do what I had to do. I was taught gotta make it, I can make it Airborne. Yes, I was getting into this Army stuff now. Once again, early wake ups but no running, no physical training, but there was (KP) Kitchen Patrol but I had that letter (W) going for me. By the time it got around to (W) the training would be over with.

    This post was a quiet spot, clean, not much traffic anywhere surrounded by Eufaula, Alabama, Decatur and Huntsville where the Post was located. This place was weird also, it had skunks and funny looking birds that flew at night but most of all it had tornadoes. They would sit down at the drop of a hat, it had only two television channels, so you saw the same thing twice a day. Plenty of the Untouchables and Car 54, Where Are You, Zorro and plenty of white boys that had never had a taste of Heroin, so I took my time introducing my product. While walking the area, as I knew I would I found the heads, it was easy here because all of the buildings were one story, long but low to the ground, no where to hide while you smoked some weed and the fumes could be smelled three to four buildings away and there wasn't any laundry service.

A laundry mat was way down the road away from the Barracks. The Officers, Sergeants wide open to sell ones wares, yea. I would make out in this little town. By the third week I was in like flint, but running out of product so on a Friday in April I rented a Chevy Impala and hit the road from Alabama to Georgia up the coast to B-more. It took 11 ½ hours. I was booking only to slow down in those little towns of a few blocks where speed traps were known to be. I had a run down on the cops hideouts, and speed traps when I hit town. What I had called ahead for was ready, a drop off of the money and a quickie with one of the drug girls and back on the road I went.

My people found out I was in town, they heard it from the grapevine, back on the road. I was as careful as a whore in church. I didn't need any cops stopping me on this trip back. When I passed that golden dome over in Georgia I began to drive easy. I made it back to the Post, hardly missed, business as usual. Now my training routine was awesome, hard as hell. I found that I had to hit and miss on my doses of my product, it was messing with my concentration and I wanted to do well. The classes had people from all over the world. Really, Africans, Mexicans, Germans, Koreans, it was all kinds a true "Heinz 57" group and I wasn't gonna be the dumbest in the class plus I must have done well on my aptitude test to get put here. These dudes were serious, but they still partied on the weekends like a bunch of fools. Anything goes was the calling from Friday night through Sunday night and I loved it.

Now, I went to demolition (explosives) messing with fuses C-4, primers and junk could kill a lot of people and especially me if I were to mess up so my head had to be on straight. I was wide-eyed and amazed to the many ways man had thought of how to kill another man. At the same time I was thinking how these same weapons would be used on my people in the event of the revolution we had been talking about for years now. Further, how if I were still in the Service would I be called upon to kill with no remorse about killing my own people (bullshit) I made my mind up that I was going to learn all I could and store it away if ever needed back home. They were going to use me so I was going to use them right back. This was my mind set for the rest of my tours in the Service.

I hit the Army pamphlets, researched documents, read all of the materials I could get my hands on along with the demo, we also studied accounting and retrograde and a little renovation of the material we were to handle. There was a lot to learn because there was a lot to having this job title. Army called job titles (MOS) and this one covered four job titles. We had to cross train, we had to become sharp, sharper than sharp. I almost felt guilty about selling junk to the guys. They had a lot to handle, trying to learn all of this stuff. I had to learn it also and I was dealing with it so what the hell. I was out to get paid! Time passed so quickly, testing began, then test after test, some lasting for hours.

My head ached from all of the testing, plus I was beginning to start to jones (withdrawals). *That man that administered these tests had better let us out of here or I'll shit right here* I was thinking. I popped up like a cork in water as I made it towards the door that led to the hallway to the stall I broke and blew the toilet away. I emptied out all at once. I felt a lot better but I lit the shit house room up. I was released on all fronts. All to do was to get off and then await for the grades to be posted. Two days passed, then the word was out, grades were posted. Gingerly, I walked up to the board. I looked up the (Ws) and there I was a 96.5% overall. I just stood there in the way, looking off into the huge plot of green grass with a huge blue skyline above. I think I felt a high like I had never felt before, may be even better than poppies couldn't touch this. Once again, the ceremony. The Star Spangled Banner, a salute and a proud, proud feeling but I also had thoughts of pounds of herb, two dollar grams of Heroin and how to get it shipped back home. This time after training, no home trip.

I was off to Kentucky and Airborne training school and if you ever saw a 1940 Paratrooper movie, it was two times harder and the Marines don't have anything on the Army. Fort Campbell, Kentucky brought the best out of me and damn near turned my head against drugs all together. There isn't much to talk about because my drug usage was next to null because all of the men were serious about being up to par to reach the standard to wear that screaming eagle patch, it carried a tradition and a lot of good men had died wearing that patch and those jump boots. After hearing and reading all of that proud but bloody history I gained a little pride and respect for the Army. But I still carried a different respect, opinion, for America's policies through history and its reasons to start or why U.S. men were involved in its wars. I started studying world history books and going to the library when I had time, especially the noncommissioned officers study materials.

Now, I'll confess I yearned to do my product but I saw and knew from the vibes, no one there was to mess up! There wasn't too much fooling around. By now we had grown, matured in months, almost changed people and I knew if I sold anyone of my fellow soldiers some junk and they got hurt, I'd have to answer to the entire Platoon Company and be hated by them all, and I was thinking ahead, I didn't want any of my GI buddies hating me in Nam. So, that old safety deposition box in Louisville was a very good move. The camaraderie was different of sorts. The Sergeants had given us a mindset of you have to learn to accept death like a lay down and a wake up, so practice it.

It took some thinking to really understand what was meant because I hadn't really experienced it yet, but between the running, physical training, field training and jumps I had all of my decisions come true, cold sober. We went to Panama for our jungle training and had a R&R (rest and relaxation) period for a four day leave, but most talk was about the war we were to go to.

PART III

THE 'NAM'

Chapter 7
To Viet Nam

Upon completion back in Kentucky and no break, Georgia Airport to California receiving station, a nine day locked in, under guard (MPs), eat, sleep, awake, wait, day to day to day when your number is called, shipped on a plane, a 24 hour flight; you land in Viet Nam. Now, I must confess, while waiting to get shipped overseas, my first look at California was from behind a double guarded gate. No GIs going overseas were allowed to roam outside of the fenced area but the other side of that huge building was the entrance for returning Vets from Nam and they were wild, some acted crazy as a loon. They had herb, hashish, little bottles of horse as it was called by some of the returning Vets. Well, after seeing how they looked and acted, I waned what they had! So, when one of the Vets threw one of those little bottles over the fence, I snatched it up and found a place to hide. This place was so wide open, finding a place to hide was a real task. I was told one could smoke this dope, no trouble, I stripped the tobacco out of the sleeve and mixed my little gift package into the powder, then refilled the sleeve, lit up, breathing in, a couple of minutes passed and I was ripped. I was looking around for some top rolling papers. I sure didn't want to waste tobacco if I didn't have to. I was going to thin those smokes out. Man, when my number finally was called, I had to be told it was up. I processed out, then to the awaiting bus to the airport and up and away. We stopped at midway, then at a place called Tan Son Nhut Airport. The place coming in, looking like a city, long building laid out, but no high rise building, a pond landing. There was a beehive of activity, airmen, soldiers, civilians all over the place. We bused to an Army Post on this very large Post, Camp Swampy Army branch and within hours, trucked to another Post called Long Bien Post. The largest Post in Southeast Asia and Viet Nam. We were sent to the reception station. The reception station was a harried place, old building, crowded as hell. The men were bitchy or stoned out of their minds, during the night. The place didn't have electricity in most of the buildings. The shit houses, man were just that! Shit houses. Morale was at an all time low in this place, some guys had been stuck here for weeks, and weeks, lost orders, no assignments. Poor record classification had them stuck here going crazy and drugging out of their minds. Now, I saw a lot of white boys, yes I thought some of them had been drafted also. A night after what was suppose to be lights out, I learned that a light on could get you killed. Ahah, that's why the building didn't have any lights inside them. This made sense, plus walking around in all of this darkness, I was seeing like a cat or was it that good herb I had been pulling up all day the Sergeant was selling us (new guys).

Now at this place we ate out of boxes, sandwiches, warm milk or fruit drinks and Twinkies. The rest of our time was spent blown away. Plenty of the guys had never gotten off (high) before and some of them seemed wilded out during the day. The air was thick with the scent of Herb, at night it looked like thousands of little fireflies popping on and off, young bodies all over the place just sitting and laying all around, nothing formal about this spot. Then there would be a call for a formation and assignment of duty stations, which was long awaited on. The Army had fooled a lot of us. We had been trained at these Army schools for certain jobs, studied and tested, and passed all of the tests given, only to find that our new assignments had not one thing to do with what we were trained for, like trained as a truck driver to be made a tower guard, or a cook or trained to be clerks now to be a motor pool monkey.

Chapter 8
Specialized Training

The Army was putting us wherever they wanted to use us doing whatever they said. These new orders sobered a bunch of us up quickly. Nam was starting off to be a trip. Now, I was crossed trained, thank you God. Explosive ordinance, renovation, retrograde and record clerking or accounting, but it all was related as to getting the job done, completed and when I was called up, none of my job tasks were changed.

I was assigned to USAVN instead of the 101st Airborne Division. The difference was USAVN was in the South of Vietnam, and 101st Airborne was up North Viet Nam, another plane ride away. But it stayed warm down here in the south I was told, and the south came with benefits I was told. What benefit I sure didn't know at that point. All I knew was I had been tricked by the Army. So the writing was on the wall, it was time to leave this place and move on, so I did. Back onto a bus and onwards, we rode and rode to this Post called Long Bien Post, it was one big spot! Man, it went on and on forever.

Soldiers were all over the place. USA soldiers, Viet Nam guys, all kinds of buildings, small Posts inside of this huge Post. This ride was showing us a lot and still we were riding to what end? We traveled so long I even forgot where the gate was when we came in the Post. Then we went up this huge hill, coming to the top, it opened to the sky and this huge valley like ridge rim. Man, as you looked down there was this huge, huge city! Building after building, it was sectioned off like a Jewish Star of David, then a huge road that led to a bunch of buildings that ran to another huge star shaped outlined group of buildings with smaller groups of buildings all about the center buildings, then an air strip behind that with motor pools and more and more buildings.

In the back, it looked as if all of the soldiers in Viet Nam was here, right here and we were part of it all, like there was not a sound heard on our bus, nothing! We were looking around at one another wide-eyed and quiet. Then a Sergeant spoke up! "Welcome to Long Bien Post, your new home boys. Welcome!" The ride from that point on revealed a lot, fellow GIs waived at the buses, saluted us, black guys raised their fist (in proud salutes) shouts, whistles came from all over. This place seemed to have it all.

There was the main street, it had three PX shops, barber shops, officers, NCO, and enlisted men clubs. There were ball courts, churches, barracks sprinkled all in between mess halls, post offices, supply stores, a real city like base. It had streetlights and giant parachuted movie outdoor houses and when you looked closely girls and more girls walking around, washing clothes, cleaning streets and doing all kinds of stuff. Some of the girls were light skinned, some dark skinned, all dressed in pajamas of all colors. My first thought I've got to get me one of them (for sure) yea! Finally, reaching our drop off stop, we unloaded our gear in front of a company quarter orderly room.

The First Sergeant and Captain came out to greet us. We then walked to our billet where we were to live for the next year and five months. This building was two stories high, wood, screened in with wooden shutters, 40 bays, and to find out we had four women per level that were assigned as our housekeepers, each of us was told to choose a roomey. Two men per bay or cube as we were to call our area. Then section off the area with walls and a door. This black guy from . Rochester, New York and I teamed up as roomeys. We went about getting our bunks, sheets, blankets, foot lockers and the rest of needed goods from the supply room. By nightfall we had out cube set up. We were worn out after the day's activities. About 1:00 a.m. all hell seemed to break lose! There were footsteps running over top of our heads, loud voices, bumping, dragging sounds on the ceiling, shouts, screams, loud, loud music. It seemed the entire company area was alive with wild goings on. The entire new guy level of our building was up and about. Now as badly as I wanted to check it out, to what the hell was going on, I didn't, being new there I didn't want to start any waves on the calm waters of this unknown waters, so I chilled.

The camp seemed so big and I knew I had to check every corner of this Post out. Now I had three days running from one place to another place. I had been about finance and compound ration cards by some of the returning Vets I had met while in my basic training school. I couldn't wait to get my hands on a few of these cards. The cards offered everything a GI could ever use anything, shoes, tennis, food, televisions, radios, watches, rings, health care goods, catalogs to order stuff from back home or from Hong Kong, the world, but the prices were two times cheaper than the USA prices and no taxes.

Now, every soldier in Nam was given a card. The thing was to have a few of them, of which I wanted! This was going to be my new hustle. I plan to buy cheap and sell high to the natives (Vietnamese people). I had heard about the black market and how it worked and I was geared up to play the market to death. Well, now my turn to fill out the form to get my ration card. A young specialist Grade 4 was to interview me. He asked a few questions and was about to pull the roll of cards from his desk. I made my move, "Say man, we don't get paid for another 21 days and everyone could use some cash, right?" He looked over at me not saying a word. I pulled out my knot of dollars from my shirt pocket, laid it carefully on his desk, then we sat there looking at one another.

He didn't call the MP that was posted up at the front door, so I knew I was in good shape. Finally, he spoke, "What do you want me to do huh?" "Well, I said I would like to have a few of those cards plus mine. "A few, he replied?" "Yea, I have American green, not that funny money, American green, meant USA currency." U.S. dollars carried two times its value overseas, but I didn't know that back then. This had this guy biting at the bit, American $100 bills. He jumped right on this proposition with both feet, he told me to come back over to this place later on this day and he would have the cards ready for me. Deal, no matter the cost I wanted these cards, each card was good for one year of buying all of the goods I could sell, to include liquor, whiskey and wine and beer also. I hadn't been told about this also. Come to find out most of the young men didn't drink.

Most of Nam was a bunch of heads. Well, I left the rational supply office happy. Now to find my way back to this place was my only worry. To make sure I found this place again I put my room/cube mate Bro. Rochester down with the deal I had just made so we could do Nam together, plus he was good with directions and he had been freelancing the Post everyday since we had been here. Later that day we made our way back to the ration office. The young white SP 4 cut us off short of getting to close the office. He had another guy with him. They both had cards and wanted $200 American green for them a piece.

I wanted three of them, Bro. Rochester wanted three also but was short, he only had $540 and change. I had plenty of cash so I kicked in for Bro. Rochester. The sight of all of the green I had got the boys all excited. They tried to offload all of the cards right there. They kept looking at the $100 bills as if they had never seen any before, holding the bills up towards the sun, turning the bills over and over again and again. This struck me strange but I didn't say anything at that time. We took our new cards and smiled as we walked away.

On our way back to our area Brothers kept on throwing kisses and funny looking smiles at Bro. Rochester and me. Now, Bro. Rochester mentioned that the Herb couldn't be that good, that all of these guys were getting off on us. Walking through a Company area, one of the Vietnamese girls called us new guys and pointed at our legs. Oh, now we got it! Our pants were not taped like the other guys we saw. This was a dead give away that we were new in the country. Well, we had to do something about this for sure!

Since we had walked back to the ration office, we saw a lot more of this Post than we had from the back of a truck. There were a lot of bunkers with guys sunbathing, playing freebies, just laying around on the ground. You could hear all kinds of music playing, country, soul, rock, blues, folk, name it you could hear it. The PX had sold a lot of record players but we saw hardly any brothers, just whites. We even began to feel wild as we walked about. The white boys were looking kind of wild at us, but no matter, we didn't know what to think. The little Vietnamese girls kept on saying something but we didn't understand any of that Vietnamese stuff, they just smiled and pointed and laughed more. Some of the girls seemed to hide from us. Others just looked like we were odd or something. Some of them were cute, some boss ugly with black stuff on their teeth. Like I said, boss ugly, but we also saw how this place was divided into different groups, like sections had groups that did different types of jobs, like MPs (police) guards that guarded the fence line, cooks, motor pool men, clerks and so on and on and then the outside group was the real soldiers, the infantrymen, helicopters, dead center of the Post was the Command Center, the big dogs. Headquarters, all of the service and supply units were spread all about. This place was beginning to make sense to us as to how it was set up. This place even had Posts inside of Posts and Long Bien Post was the mother area made up of a lot of Posts and airstrips and ammo depots of which we had not seen yet. Because we hadn't started to work yet, Bro. Rochester and I took every new sight in one at a time trying to learn what we had been thrown into.

Now, Bro. Rochester was from Rochester, New York but I still until today think NY by way of South Carolina because he had a southern drawl that he carried with talking so fast. Most of the time I understood the Vietnamese better than I did him. He was a good guy, he didn't drink, smoke nor did he cuss, but was he death on the chicks! Yes! He liked the girls but only one at a time. I think he had some church up in him, he had morals and things, but I was to help him change all of that stuff. With time he would change and be a good homeboy. As we walked, we talked about upstairs at our billet, upstairs where all of the noise, yelling, loud music and dragging stuff across the floor was going on up there. We made a pack to check it out when we got back to our cube. Regardless of those white boys, so that night when the whoop lie started, we ventured up the stairs. At the top of the stairs we faced a sign that stated, "Stay out!" Well, that didn't mean us, we entered!

Inside there was cube after cube, all had doors, blue red, green, and yellow light bulbs in the ceilings. The doors had peace signs and all kind of stuff painted on them. In the middle of the bay was of all things a ping pong table, speakers hung from the middle beam in the ceiling, a refrigerator, a long bench, a set of drums, two guitars, mic with speakers, strove light, a huge television over in one corner and they had a yellow dog up there, the dog had a dog house up here too. A basketball hoop, ball, bats, a rack of baseballs, two footballs, tennis rackets, volleyballs, Frisbees up the ass and a bunch of naked women posted all about the walls and posts. This place was cool! So, that's what's been going on up here, fun. Real run of the mill fun, with the yellow dog barking like it had never seen black men before some one hollered, " Savage shut up, shut up, Bitch!" Then a door opened and a white boy looked out of the door, he looked stirred, then stumbled out of the cube, "Can I help you guys, he asked?" Our reply, "No." "Well, what do you want up here in this billet bro?" Rochester said "We live here too, downstairs." "Oh, so you are the new guys. Well, welcome!" "I am Stewart, Spec-5." Bro. Rochester spoke on, "Walker and I'm Bro. Rochester. "PFCs," we laughed. The dude motioned us to sit on the bench, we did. How long in the country? "A week," Bro. Rochester spoke. "How do you like Nam, don't judge, take tee-tee time to like it much, you'll see." "See, I speak Gook."

This was the first time I heard Gook and I didn't like the sound of it. It sounded like a come down, something degrading about the way he said it, but he could say what he wanted to. Who was I to judge? Bro. Rochester knew how I felt and later he told me that word meant nigger. That opening statement I carried with me through my entire tour of Nam and I never allowed any one else to say "Gook" without me saying something about it!

Back to Stewart, he had done one tour already and was months into his second tour. Bro. Rochester and I looked at one another thinking this guy is a nut, we soon found out almost all of the guys in this unit had 2 and 3 tours under their belts working in this same unit and most of all these soldiers had rank, Spec 6 and Spec 7, upper ladder soldiers in this man's Army and they were all young like us.

Nam was the place to make rank. By now there was a couple of other guys had stuck their heads out of their cubes, two whites and I thought one black but he didn't consider himself black come to find out, he was from the

West Indies named Jesus. He was black but didn't know it: Damn fool, I thought. He looked us up and down, then went back into his cube *fuck him* I thought *fuck him*. The two white guys acted cool, offered us a *Jay* (reefer), turned on the record player, even offered to play a game of ping pong and then got us a couple of cokes. We talked and talked until the rest of the crew got in. They came into the billet with a ½ case of three flavors ice cream. We ate and blew a few *Jays* or shall I say I blew *Jays* with them. Man, I was ripped, this was my first *Jay* since the reception center and the Herb was good, it was almost daylight when Bro. Rochester and I went downstairs.

I slept until lunchtime that day. Bro. Rochester was up and gone as usual. I awoke to hear a low singing voice, a female voice at the far end of our floor billet was this little room. In it were two ironing boards, wash basins, a small radio, mirror, three stools, a fridge, and cardboard, space and picture after pictures of GIs.

In the room, a little Vietnamese woman and then another woman came in the door from outside; two of them dressed in pajamas with little flowers on them. The one that had just opened the door, taller and better looking had my full attention, plus she had no underwear on under those pajamas. I could see right through them with the sun shining at her back. She noticed me looking and just smiled and lowered her head and smiled. The shorter woman laughed and said something in Vietnamese and punched me on my arm and shook her head and pointed her finger at me.

I just stood there, with my eyes on her girlfriend. The little woman looked at me and in broken English said "Mein Dan Walker, yes?" I didn't know what to say, she spoke English and could read it too. She knew my name, but how? She pointed to my name tag on my shirt, that's how dummy, I thought. "Yes Walker," the taller woman said "Cholin" and pointed to herself, "Cholin, I replied.

The little one said Cho Kim, Kim and Lin laughing and we laughed together. "You live Number 4 cube, yes." Kim said. "Yes," I replied after counting where our cube was located. "We do for you, you and friend too", Kim said. "Oh me and Bro. Rochester" "Bro. Rochester?" both women said together, "Yes". "Bro. Rochester friend to me," I replied.

We had broken the ice with small talk but I wanted to know about this Mein Dan thing or whatever it was. Was Mein Dan good or bad, but I would have to find out later on because I had to shower up and get to finding out where Bro. Rochester had gone. So, I gathered my shower stuff and walked down the makeshift sidewalk to the showers and shithouse. I opened the door, steam jumped out at me. I walked in, the joint was full of women! Vietnamese women and piles of clothes, they were washing the GIs uniforms in the showers. They were soaking wet, soap all over the floor, women on their knees, all soaped down we with those extra thin pajamas on. All of their body shapes could be seen, the pajamas were skin tight. I liked the way they washed clothes honest, I did! I looked onward only to see men! Yes, men in here showering like the women weren't even here and the women acted the same with them.

An older woman came forward and reached past me to shut the opened door, flicked her hand as if to tell me to move. So, I did. She flicked me over to a running shower and motioned me to shower up so, I dropped my shorts, hung my towels, grabbed some soap and began to wash.

No one was shy and I was enjoying looking and lusting on their wet pajama bodies. Man was I lusting. Thank God for the cold water. I made my mind up. I was going to shower at this time of the day from then on. When I returned to my billet. Lin the tall one whispered something to Kim, the small one and they laughed out loud. Kim asked "Walker, you wash, yes?" and laughed, "Yes," I said. I had both of my hands up spreading my fingers, this many girlfriends wash Walker. The woman really got a kick out of my saying that.

I dressed and couldn't wait to tell Bro. Rochester about my new adventure and when I did see him and told him what had happened, he thought I was still high from the night before. I finally got the boy Stewart to verify that the women did wash clothes in the showers and how they didn't care who was in there doing whatever in there but added it would cost a couple of bucks, and he did mean a couple of bucks only. As we would find out as the days went on. This struck me as being swell! For I had seen Lin and I wanted her already.

Well, Bro. Rochester and I had almost got comfortable when our first Sunday came in Nam, but we knew Monday was coming and work had to start. Like any other soldier, we made ready for the day. All set to shine my boots up, and they were missing, both pair of my new boots. I was hot, as usual Bro. Rochester was not to be found. I checked outside on the bottom stair landing. There was about twenty pairs of boots. The girls were squatted, working the hell out of brushes. Spit shinning the boots. I found out boots was a part of their cleaning jobs also. They were to do all the things we soldiers use to do and they did it with a smile on their faces.

I had to find out all I could about these women and the other women who were to do for us. Well, Bro. Rochester knew a lot more than me about the Post, the women and what was going on around here because he was always out, talking to people even though I didn't understand how people could understand him and his country ass, but they did. So, I questioned him on a regular. Bro. Rochester filled me in on most of the guys in this Unit.

The rumors of who was slamming who as far as the housekeepers went. He told me Stewart had Lin as his woman a year back and she had loved him (too much). The dummy blew her by giving her the "clap". He had corn holed her and everything. Stewart was a real freak. He also had been slamming two other housekeeping women at the same time and that's how he had got the "clap". This messed me up, shit! I had dug that chick and she had to belong to a white guy. Bro. Rochester said she wouldn't mess with another GI no matter what! Also, Kim had gone with a couple of white boys that had already gone home after their tours and she was married to a South Vietnamese man and had two kids for him and he knew he made her whore around to get the GI's money every month. Bro. Rochester told me all of the housekeepers had a price. All we had to do was to pay and that's why they were there for us. There were hundreds of them on this Post. That night I was educated by my roomey and now armed with a lot of knowledge. Bro. Rochester also told me he knew where to get our pants done so we wouldn't look like new guys for only $2.00 a pair and I had to see the sewing lady. "Wow," he yelled, "Wow".

Well, Monday came and we got into a truck, me, Bro. Rochester and two other white soldiers. We rode for about ten minutes, looking out the back of the truck. We saw buses, bus stops, street signs, then a long road. This road had buildings that looked like downtown in some USA city. They had air condition, long lawns with women cutting grass with pointed straw hats on in those pajamas. There were larger buildings, 10 or 15 stories high with Jeeps parked in parking lots with crosswalks.

We stopped and jumped off the truck in front of this extra big building that went on for blocks and blocks, turned a corner and went on and on. This was Headquarters and Headquarters USAV Long Bien Post! This was where Bro. Rochester and I was to work from HQ & HQ USAV Desk Log Long Bien Post, Viet Nam. This building housed General Stevenson a four-star General of the Army of Viet Nam. He was in charge of every soldier in South Viet Nam and we had lucked up to be working in the same building with the General and his staff. Boy! This was too much. "No getting killed here", Bro. Rochester said, "We're safe from the war Brother Walker, safe".

In we went, we were stopped by four MPs just inside the doorway, motioned to a desk. There we gave a Sergeant our orders to station papers. He looked them over, pointed to another desk. There was a camera set up there, we had our pictures taken, then our fingers printed, then they made us badges and gave us little ID cards for our wallets. The Sergeant that brought us there waited for us, then he directed us to some elevators. We went to the fifth floor and got off. We had to show our ID at a desk then the door opened to a huge room filled with soldiers all over the place.

We followed the Sergeant across one room to another until we reached an inner room. This room had all kinds of bullets, motors, shells, claymore mines, 105 and 155 canisters all about. This looked like one of the classrooms back in Alabama, Redstone Arsenal Training School. This had to be our workroom. Every head in the room turned our way as we just stood there in awe. A Captain came forward but walked right pass us. He was visiting, I guessed. Then a Major came toward us. He said "Welcome troops, I'm Major Thomas, your boss." He went on to say how lucky we were to work for him and the U.S. Army in this here war in Viet Nam. He told us he didn't put up with any shit! He stated he didn't care where we came from, or who we liked or disliked, needed, wanted, loved or hated. He just wanted us to perform as soldiers and respect the Military Code of Justice and honor the U.S. Army ways. Then he walked away. He made a hell of a first impression. Then a small white headed man came forward, he was a *full bird* Colonel, that's just below a one-star General. This man smiled and shook our hands, told us to follow him into an office. We sat. The *Full Bird* talked slowly and low.

He told us of the mission of this detachment for we were not really part of the Company. We were in support of many companies, both North and South Viet Nam supporters. We were the 182nd EOD (Ordnance and Ammo Despot Liaison Detachment Unit) for HQ, HQ USAV, Long Bien Post and MACV HQ Saigon, Viet Nam. We were to ride high over all of the Ammo Despots in Viet Nam. We were responsible for EOD storage requisition, retrograde, renovation, and recordkeeping of all of the bombs, bullets and be-be all over Viet Nam.

This was serious stuff! And to boot, there was only 35 men in charge of all of this stuff and we were just 2 of the 35 men. We were to work on our own. We would have individual assignments to complete. We would not have any officers over us. Only the Major could change our assignment. After talking to him, the *Full Bird* would change the assignment. No one had any time to miss from work, no sick calls, come in sick, but come in and work. We were to have top secret clearances to top secret information as to shipment of ammunition orders and shipments to Nam and back to the USA. We also monitored top secret information on what weapons we destroyed and new weapons tried out on our enemies.

Our job was one of killing, a job that was one to save us soldiers and its allies in this war. The *Full Bird* was straight to the point, he made our mission real. The *Full Bird* laid the law down. He talked on for about three hours nonstop. When we got out of his office we were ready to kick ass! This man made me feel like a real American, proud, brave, fearless and much more airborne than I had ever felt. I was ready to do my job or try to anyway. Plus, he told us we would be traveling all over Nam to do our job, that's why we had so much ID and each of us was to be treated like officers by every other officer in this man's Army. They had to respect our skills, we represented and we were part of his hilltop staff for the North and South of all of Viet Nam.

We were the can do bunch and no one in this outfit was a lower grade than Spec 5 which was Sergeant. Yes, Spec 5. Bro. Rochester, me and the two white guys would all have Spec 5 stripes after one month of working this HQ & HQ USAV Desk Log Ammo. Man, this was too much! I was beginning to grow again. I had to beat the books again, there was a lot to learn, a lot of new stuff to master, a lot of people I didn't know needed me to be good at this job to help save their lives. Bro. Rochester and I studied all night, a lot of nights. We tested one another over and over even though the men in this Unit smoked a lot of Herb and they partied damn near every night, they did their jobs.

Soon Bro. Rochester and I were accepted into the entire scheme of things. They invited us to their pot parties and passed on information they were assigned. We were a unit counting on one another. For almost 4 months we worked and studied like students in school all over again and it had paid off. Without any problem, the Army had changed me.

Bro. Rochester, he was already to be changed. I was so busy, I had forgot all about a hustle, my ration cards, the chicks, man was I changed. I was so busy I had not even written home to my mom, sisters and brothers so I set out to catching up on my writing home. I had forgotten about all of my plans of sending lots of money home each week from selling products over here thus far. I had not seen too many guys doing Heroin, just reefers.

There didn't seem to be a demand for the hard stuff. Most of my letters were about the welfare of the family, with a great deal of interest of what my young fresh sisters were up to? The girls had just noticed boys, especially the oldest girl Delnora. She was entering junior high school, a good looking, built like a brick shithouse, black child. She indeed bared watching but I had left Noddie, my brother and next in age to me to watch over her. Also there was *Ma*, who would cut her off at the waist if Del messed up. The two younger girls I knew were still little girls, they would be ok. Larry, my youngest brother, well he was quiet, shy like, small in stature. He would come into his own like all of the rest of the young boys around the way. That's the way I saw it anyway. And that's about how my letters went.

But still new in the country and with a lot to learn about this place, I had time to get my hustle on. I had not lost sight on my retirement at 45 years old. Oh no! Never. One way I knew to scope the waters out about what? How much? And what the GIs were smoking, shooting or what not was to have my scout check things out.

My man and roomey Ole Bro. Rochester, was the traveling man. If anyone could find out what was up, Bro. Rochester could. So, I kind of put my plan to work. Bro. Rochester and his country self got along well with all of the white boys, may be a lot of white s lived in upstate New York or something, but for sure no white s lived near where I had come from back in Baltimore on the Westside of town (for sure). Well, right off Bro. Rochester put me down with most of the soldiers on this Post didn't live like us. What? What do you mean, all he said was I had to take a long walk with him one of these nights. This peaked my interest. I felt I had to take this walk just for the look see. This thought stayed with me for a couple of days and then we were ready to do it. Once again, I was wide open for anything.

We walked down from the hill where we lived out of sight from the brick building. The area seemed to change the further we walked. No streetlights, crosswalks, then the roads got rough looking and you could feel the rocks and stones under foot. The buildings got to looking bad also. Some makeshift ball courts with straw baskets just like the ones back home and the brothers live here, brothers upon brothers. Blacks up the ling-ling all over the place. The men looked kind of hard, no pressed uniforms here, no shined boots (no sir) towels draped around the neck, black armbands, black wrist bracelets, neck bones and pig-foot bones on shoestrings draped around their necks, they had dark sunglasses on and it was pitch black out here. No one was saying anything to one another as they met. The just walked up to one another and started to slapping hands together.

Some of the brothers rocked as they slapped hands, then slapped one another arms and some motioned to cut their own throats upon finishing all of the slapping and stuff. One guy even added stomping his feet in the dirt under his feet. It seemed these men were mad about something or at somebody. We got some funny looks from most of the guys with me especially staring like a fool to what I was seeing for the first time. I had to find out what this was all about.

Bro. Rochester had not let on to any of these events coming off. It was for me to learn. I found out later. Some of the GIs seemed tickled as they looked at us with our brand new, fresh looking uniforms and shiny boots and these tired ass baseball caps we wore. These guys had green slouch bucket hats, that had all kinds of stuff hanging on them, but I was impressed by the use of the shoestring. Those black shoe strings had been made into black crosses wrist bands, bucket hat bands, arm bands, pant legs bloused tightly, dog tag chains, eyeglass arm extensions and they were just plain slick. How could they see with those dark sunglasses on at night? Damn nearly everybody had sunglasses on at night as a white boy would say *far out!*

As we walked on, I smelled weed, rich good weed. If you smoked, you knew good weed when you smelled it. This was real good weed. I was smelling it (no doubt).

Then something else, what? Yes! I know that smell, that's Heroin, yes Herron-Herron!

I saw the fireflies twinkling on and off as it was inhaled. Some brothers were smoking dope. Now, I had blew some Herron back in California. I knew what time it was. So this is where this town came together. Down here or over here, whatever, here! Yea, ouch! I damn near broke my leg stumbling over something I couldn't see in all of this darkness but I didn't go down so I'm ok.

Bro. Rochester led me to this building, wooden, raggedly, the windows had holes in the screen and it smelled like sweat and stinky feet. The joint also smelled like piss. Inside we saw no lights but a record was playing somewhere in here. The faint outline of bunks and people walking and sitting around. The first flies flickering on and off and the thick smell of Herron - Herron. Bro. Rochester calls out "Gary, Gary, it's me Bro. Rochester," "Who?" was asked from the darkness. "Bro. Rochester, don't know no one here know no Bro. Rochester." Bro. Rochester answered, "Somebody here had better know this Bro. Rochester," and began to laugh.

From the darkness came a shape, a tall, dark figure formed. This guy was Bro. Rochester's cuz and more so to my surprise Bro. Rochester began to slapping hands with his cuz. It was a short slapping session but he did it. Bro. Rochester knew one of those slapping things (yea, he had to teach me how to do that also). My man Bro. Rochester, a common bastard didn't tell me nothing about all of this stuff! The two began to celebrate one another the minute in time together for that instance I think everybody in that dark funky building could feel the love.

Bro. Rochester introduced me to his cuz Gary, he lit his zippo lighter to take a look at me, then put out his balled up fist. At first I just stood there, Gary looked at Bro. Rochester and said "You haven't taught the brother how to dapt yet?" Dapt, so that's what that slapping is called, Dapt. "Dapting," Gary told me to make a fist, he bumped his fist to mine twice, then said open your hand, slap three times, then grab my hand squeeze it and then bump fists again, then snap your fingers. I did it, that's Dapt brother. I felt sure enough an Airborne soldier ready to pick up a gun.

As this was going on I was so into it I didn't even notice three other brothers had lit their lighters to light the room for us to see and be seen. Well, Bro. Rochester and Gary talked and talked. I sat in the darkness practicing my Dapt by myself. Gary laughed and said "Man, you will have plenty of time to get good at Dapt (don't sweat it). I sat there thinking, I'm getting blessed tonight (real). I have found the Blacks, where the town comes together, learned Dapt, and some home guy slang and I wonder if I'll ever get to come back here? Because I sure didn't know where in the hell I was. Bro. Rochester broke up my thoughts, we have to go and we left. While walking, I told Bro. Rochester he wasn't shit! He could have told me about all of this, he answered, "Now you know, that was good enough for me".

As we walked back, I tried to remember every step back to our cube. My mind was churning, why such a change in the way we were living on the same post? Why was there such a difference in attitudes among us soldiers over here? It seemed that the same things that were going on at home were going on over here, but we were all Americans. We had a foe to fight but race was a factor. I was not really surprised but I was expecting something different. Bro. Rochester and I talked as we walked back. A new respect for Bro. Rochester was forming in my mind. He was smart and knew how to play the game. I would use a page out of the same book he was using to get by. Not getting lost in the role cause I still had to be me.

With this new information, I began to notice little things within my Unit, there were three groups. The laid back, Bro. Rochester, me, white boy, black Jesus, and two white boys, real white boys John and Charles. Stewart and Charles were from California. They couldn't help but be cool, they were from Cali. John was from New York City. He knew about Blacks. The second group was a bunch of fools from the deep south, Alabama, Georgia, Virginia, cold ass Minnesota, Wyoming, Texas and (I do mean Ass-Texas), Connecticut, Boston, Massachusetts. As far as I was concerned, they were KKK. They disliked the Blacks, Mexicans, Indians, anybody who had color to their skin, but these devils were always trying to get tans, sitting in the hot sun burning up and breaking out with skin sores all over their bodies. They looked like they had chicken pox and always playing country western music.

Our third group Bro. Rochester and I called them *Creeps*. They would start breathing hard and deep whenever we were near like they couldn't breath or the air got bad when we were in close to them and they made sure not to make eye contact. Bro. Rochester and I made an oath to knock any of them out the first chance we got for any infraction we could come up with like just being in Nam would have been a good reason. Plus, it seemed that both of our enemy groups didn't want us to get tight with the housekeepers. They didn't know it but they empowered us for we knew they were really scared shitless of black men.

But as we knew, the Army was the white man's thing and we had to jell or die. So, we had to play the game 60-40 just to exist. Now, there is a saying to be forewarned is to get forearmed and we were ready for bear, big bears like grizzly. Bro. Rochester and I got even tighter now. We watched each other's backs more. What I knew, he knew. What he saw and heard, I knew about it. We even shared our mail with one another. I knew his family members, girlfriend, his likes and dislikes. I acted so funny styled. Bro. Rochester just took me day for day. The drugs and my wild ass thinking kept something going on. But he stayed my stick man. The both of us were changing. Nam had us and we were to be dead with almost 6 months in Nam. Jesus, our white/black West Indian brother man let us in on something. See, Jesus worked nights at the office and had days off while we worked day light but he was never around when we got off from work.

Well, Jesus had a secret, this dude spoke plenty of Vietnamese, he would be laughing and talking with the housekeepers all of the time when he was around but he also would be missing. This dude come to find out was going off Post! Yes, off Post! Damn near everyday after work and he was going downtown, downtown Saigon, Yes Saigon City. He was riding the troop buses and trucks that carried whatever to downtown Saigon. He had a girlfriend down there, she had a house or apartment where he stayed. He said he would take us with him to see the real Viet Nam and its people. Now even Bro. Rochester was up for this but how? When?

We made arrangements to go on a Sunday after Jesus had got off from that Saturday night he had to work (Yea). Well, it was here, we were ready, willing and wide-eyed to see all we could see of Saigon City. To the loading docks at Quarter Master (Supplies Headquarters Supply Unit) truck after truck being loaded, also a bus station, there we walked towards the bus station. Jesus reached and pulled out his ID. Well, we had ID also, so we pulled ours. Jesus flashed his ID, we flashed ours. He walked on, so did we. Jesus asked where the trucks were going, New Port. New Port I heard, didn't know what or where it was but New Port seemed to be alright. "Is there room for three bloods?" Jesus asked? "Yep," was the reply. We waited until the truck was filled. Come to find out this truck and many more were going to New Port.

Finally, I figured it out, this was a convoy, a nice size one at that. Shouts rang out, motors started, and on our way we were. The driver and his shotgun man was in the front of the truck. We three were stuffed in the back with all of these boxes. A rough ride back with all of these boxes, a rough ride but who was complaining. I could see much dust jumped up from the ground making a dust cloud. We hit every bump, hit every hole in the road. This driver must have been looking to make this a rough ride for us and he did. After an half hour or so, I smelt fish or the smell of fish, it was salt water. We were near the water all right, New Port. That's just what it was a New Port. The US Army had drugged the water away to make the Port extend more inland to form a New Port here.

There were hundreds of huge buildings, tractor and trailer and all kinds of GIs, Army, C-Bees, Sailors, Marines, Vietnamese workers. This place was full of activity. The trucks stopped. Soon a MP pulled the end tarp up on the back of the truck where we sat. The MP asked for ID. We flashed our dog tags, and ID cards. No problem.

We jumped off the truck following Jesus to some funny looking motorcycles that had a bucket like cabin with a seat and top tarp on it. The driver, a small Vietnamese man smoking a cigarette, wearing a pointed straw hat with short pants on and a dirty off white shirt and some really wild thick, black sandals on. He spoke "Where you go Soul?" "Soul," he said with a cheese eating ass smile on his face. "Saigon," Jesus said. The man looked, counted on his fingers three, peeping around Jesus to see Bro. Rochester and me standing behind Jesus. He hollered something out to another driver of the dumb looking motorcycle. The man started his machine up. Boy! The engine was boss! This thing was a monster! It had to be ready! Jesus stepped into the first man's buggy, flipped his finger backwards for Bro. Rochester and me to jump aboard the one in the back.

We jumped into number two buggy. Now, we would see everything and I do mean everything. The road was full with trucks, old cars, motorcycles and bicycles looking like motorcycles. These Vietnamese rode with whole families on one motorcycle. They carried everything on these little motorbikes and girls, man, hundreds of girls riding these bikes. There were no rules to driving in this country. There couldn't have been, but there seemed to be an understood order to things. No accidents, no street signals, no police but miles and miles of vehicles on both sides of the road and get this, no speed limit.

Now, I knew the Army convoys didn't stop for anything but where in the hell these people were going puzzled me like I had been to New York plenty of times and big crowds were nothing to me but this was a bit much! Millions of Vietnamese all over the place. I could not see pass all of the people. People carrying buckets, dogs, chickens, children. Now, I hadn't seen any kids at all until now, but there were kids over here (would you believe that). Yea. This road was a trip.

The further we rode, the more we saw them coming up to a rise. There it was a city, a very huge city, large buildings, old but huge. Store fronts for miles and miles. People dressed in native dress. The silk black pants and white blouses or shirts, sandals, umbrellas, pointed straw hats or all black colored silk outfits. Some with pretty yellow, red, light green, blue and some orange Chinese Suzy Wong like long tight formfitting dresses. These women were small, built, shapely, cute, clean looking and showed they had jobs. One could tell also the kept women that most GIs had fitted them with western style outfits. They sported hot pants, jeans, high heeled pointed shoes, long and short cut hairstyles and had sassy walks where they strutted their stuff trying to get attention, but one thing for sure, we were told no hand holding, hugging or showing affection with an American or one not of Viet Nam was tolerated by the law of Viet Nam. The woman would go to jail for showing any signs of affection in public and the foreigner would have the hell beat out of him by the Vietnamese people. So it was kept out of sight, out of mind kind of thing.

There was enough women for a man to choose a new one with every step he could take, all of their men were in the Army and were called to duty at the drop of a hat so the playing field was wide open, as long as you (GIs) had a buck and the girls knew the power they had to earn that buck. The going price was a $2.00 American. The ratio was 18 to 1 dollars when converted from U.S. dollars to Piasters or South Viet Nam dollars.

So us GIs were like millionaires to them or having Boo-Ku Rich (very, very rich). Bro. Rochester and I looked at one another and just smiled. Man, this place was nothing but a good time to come! As we went on and on the streets, it became crowded, Army trucks of all kinds ¼, ½ , 1 Ton, 3 Ton, 5 Ton, tractor trailers, name it and hundreds of jeeps could be seen. We were close to the Embassy of all of the allies of this war and the capitol house of Viet Nam. MPs up the hiney. Now, we saw Vietnamese soldiers, plenty of them, they wore real dark green fatigues. Ours was more of a drab green. They wore slick sandals and most of them didn't wear hats. If to see one with a hat, it would be an officer, not an unlisted man. Weird enough a lot of the enlisted men were women. In this country, this war all of the people did a sting in defense of their country the boys and the girls alike. They all had skills, not sissies like American girls, but they were all females believe me!

After passing the inner city, we headed to the outskirts. There we saw a long, long fence line start. This fence line was the outer limits of the largest Air Force Post/Base in South Viet Nam, Tan Son Nhut. Yes, Tan Son Nhut Air Force Base. This place made Atlanta and New York Airports look like midgets, it had 6- 8 different Posts within its perimeter and it was the entry and debarkation for the troops from all over North and South regions of Viet Nam war zones for USA troops in the country. There you would eat off of plates, have four different chow lines, choose what menu you might want, and they had showers with running hot water all day long.

The men got to change into civilian clothes after their day's tour of work. They could also go off of the Post to the inner city any time they wanted after their work tour and they had the main road that led to the strip. Plantation Road was the pathway to Sodom and Gomorrah, trick heaven, the big slippery slide way. Penny, nickel, dime, a quarter Headquarters. This road was known by every soldier in Nam. Some men had dreams of this road, wished their tour was down south here so they could visit this road and just to think Bro. Rochester and me were here, just our luck, I guess. Ha Ha Ha!

Jesus was in charge and he was leading us to his house. We rode on then. We began to see some large fort looking long gates, the walls stretched higher than five or six stories. They had some strange symbols on the front of them, to find out they were the addresses in Vietnamese. Some had American signs on them also, signs stating ("GIs stay out of this area," "Enter at your own risk!" This seemed serious and it was, we would learn about why later. So a few blocks onwards we make a right hand turn down a street. Jesus yells "Won, Quam Dinn, home!" Midway down this street, we stop. Jesus jumps out of the motorcycle cab. We follow. We stand in front of a two story pale yellow building. There was a tower like thing with a man sitting up there in a little room, to the right of the tower, a huge wooden gate, but we could see a beautiful garden behind the gate, then there seemed to be a landing with several doorways.

    We entered the gate, Jesus nodded to the armed man in the tower as we passed. We entered the middle door, then the doorway into this room that looked like it was right out of a <u>Good Housekeeping</u> magazine, potted flowers, mirrors, sofa, chairs, rugs like from Egypt or some place. There was sterling silver and a huge birdcage with three singing birds in it. The room went on into an open court that had no roof and no ceiling. You could look up and see the sun. A sunroom like, there were wicker chairs, a fountain with running water, an outside looking barbeque oven, a long table along side of it with side walls to the surroundings and to the right a cubby hole like doorway. It had stairs when you looked up a second floor spinned around the rest of the inside interior with four doorways. This place was badd! And to think Jesus said it was his! Impressed, oh yeah I was. Bro. Rochester was hunching me so hard my ribs were aching like crazy. Then Jesus Bay-Bee a woman voice broke the silence, it was Jesus' girlfriend, Lan. Lan was slim, extra slim, skinny, pale, short haircut, loud, half Chinese, half Vietnamese, talked broken English in a very high pitch. This girl was jazzy. It seemed she had hung around the USO one day too many. The woman thought she was 1/3 American also and it seemed she never shut up, but after 4 hours with her, she seemed to wear on you. She was a goodhearted person and she was really into Jesus. Jesus said he picked her up downtown near the USO one day when he was changing up U.S. dollars to Viet Nam Piaster to get that good ratio of 18 to 1 odds. She talked her way into his life and he loved her, he also had got this house for her and it would be totally hers when he left Nam for good. He also said she would be said to be rich by Viet Nam standards then.

Also, he stated he prayed that he didn't knock her up before then, cause she would kill him before she would allow him to go and leave her and a baby here. This troubled me to hear this but I filed that statement away in my mind. Jesus had gone out while Lan had been a great host to Bro. Rochester and me. He returned with a basket with all kind of veggies and a bottle of Cognac and a huge pile of chicken. He plopped it down on the long table near the outside barbeque like oven. He told Lan to get to work, patting her on her skinny but. She loved that, he walked over to this bush like tree, reached in and opened a hidden cabinet, it was full of all kinds of glasses. He blew in one as if to blow dust out of it and smiled. He reached in the cabinet again, came out with a huge sugar bowl that had reefer in it filled to the top. He had a Sherlock Holmes looking smoking pipe he stuffed with the Herb and lit it.

The smell of Herb filled the garden space. We started to passing around the pipe. The Herb was good. Soon we were relaxed, laughing wildly, sipping on the Cognac liquor, then interrupted by Lan. Lan had cooked up a storm, sweet potato, rice, green pepper, squash, sprouts, beans, onions, little peas, some red leafy stuff, eggs scrambled in with chicken and a sweet but tangy sauce. It was really on the money, also a lemonade type cold drink. Being stoned and hungry made this even better. Not much was said during the meal, it was all about eating.

Darkness was coming on, a lot of people were now coming out. It was cooler at night and the night people were about to take over the City. Jesus took Lan to the side, she disappeared only to come back with four friends, four girls. They came into view, young good looking. They seemed to be about 18 - 20 years old, quiet, shy, dressed in white blouses and dark blue pants. They had flip flop sandals on, long flowing black air with deep brown eyes and those pants rode nice on their butts! I had disrobed the four of them already. Jesus called out their names, Mai, Chao, Lee-Lin and Him. I really didn't care what their names were, I had a pocket full of cash I thought!. I'll take all four of them! Lan stepped in the middle of the girls, they whispered together, then two of the girls backed off. The other two women just stood there smiling with their heads hung low. "Ok," Jesus said. "Choose which one you want Nate." This was the first time he had called me Nate. I studied for ½ a second and chose the shorter of the two girls. She looked good to me. I pointed in her direction and she moved in on me, not saying a word, her head still hung low. I peeped down at her and softly lifted her head, up came her head with a smile on her face. I allowed a sigh out, she was really cute, sort of cat like eyes with light eye brows, a cute little nose, sort of black like, almost perfect lips and nice round breasts.

As I looked down her blouse, it was my next move so I reached out taking her elbow and led her to two chairs over to our right hand side. We almost sat down when I said, "Walker," pointing to my self. She said "Chao", "Chao," I replied, she shook her head yes. We smiled at one another. Bro. Rochester was over there doing almost the same thing. Lan, Jesus's girl said something in Vietnamese. Jesus laughed and the woman seemed to blush. Lan turned on the radio, Radio Viet Nam.

The spokesperson Saigon Sal heard all over Nam spun the records during the daylight hours until dust. The Blowfly was a brother, that carried the truth about Nam, told it as it was! He told about attacks on U.S. troops, death counts, letters from the troops, letters received from the USA and a warning from the Viet Cong and Northern Vietnamese soldier telling us to go home or die messages, his sign off call was "And Phu Bia is alright tonight." If no attack was anticipated in the upper North of Viet Nam according to U.S. information, meaning one could get a good nights sleep. Phu Bia is alright tonight was always good news, it meant they had not broken thru our defenses. Aside from the warning and news, Blowfly played music straight from California's Top 20 list and Motown's Top 10 and not to mention country western every third record, only the best of country, like Johnny Cash.

Everyone liked Johnny Cash, he told some hell of stories. Chao and I were getting along swell even though we weren't saying anything. It was about 8:30 p.m. or so when Jesus said "Well, Bro. Rochester you sleep up there, Nate you sleep up there," pointing to the rooms above our heads and then Lan and him made their way towards the stairway to the rear of where we were all sitting. Bro. Rochester moved with his girl following close.

I got up, looked at Chao and off we stepped in the same direction to the room, opened the door. Inside the light switch, on, then we could see a wardrobe, huge bed, dresser with a pitcher and huge bowl like dish, soap, towels, brush, bush comb and bush picks, a small window to the rear and a huge ceiling fan above the bed moved very slowly. Chao moved slowly toward the bed, stopped just short of the bed, turned and said in very god English, "Walker, you boyfriend me?" "Huh?" I said, "You boyfriend me Chao?" I thought, then said "Yea." I guess for sure? "You boyfriend me?" I didn't know how to answer and I sure didn't want her to walk out on me so I said "Yea." She smiled and sat on the bed, whew relieved I was. I walked pass her and the bed to the small window and peeped as if to look out of it. Chao laughed and stretched out on the bed. I stood there just looking at her. She then patted on the mattress for me to come sit, so I walked over and sat. She kneeled up and reached out taking her hands and started to rub my neck. Her hands were soft but strong, she had skills, my neck was loving this. Chao somehow got me to slip out of my shirt and tee shirt. She even unlaced my boots and took off my socks.

By now we were quite comfortable with one another. All of her movements were slow, direct and her eyes stayed glued to mine. She started mumbling something as she worked me over, over and over. I heard her saying the same thing over and over without me even noticing Chao was undressing even though she hardly seemed to had moved inches apart from me. She half turned me towards her front when I saw that her blouse, bra and pants were off and only these sweet pink panties were on her sweet but. Well, from there we did our thing. Being small and easy to move around she was a treat for me, but she made a move on me the second time. We threw down and flipped on top of me, she squatted above me, mounted and reared back and rocked, whipping her body like a slingshot. This chick was gone. She was enjoying this, she played with her long hair, reached for me with open arms and reared back and then thrust forwards again and again.

This chick really had skills after being spent, I coasted off to sleep only to be awaken by the feel of being wet. I thought I had pissed in the bed. No, I hadn't, Chao was washing me down as I slept. Still she whispered this strange but soft sounding statement that she had repeated again and again. I just laid there and enjoyed the bath. I slept with Chao in my arms. Her hair smelled like coconut oil, her skin was cool and soft. The next thing I knew, Jesus was hollering, "Put your feet on the floor men." I rolled out of the right side of the bed. I was alone, Chao had gone, left and only God knew when because I sure didn't. I felt so used but relieved in a way. No goodbye to be given up, just go back to work as usual, so we made ready to get back to Long Bien Post. On the ride back nothing was said by any of us being 4:30 a.m. It was cold, not cool but cold! I was glad to be sitting next to another warm body, but I thought how nice it would be if Bro. Rochester were Ms. Chao. Yea, that's what I was going to call her if to ever see her again. Ms. Chao, she had a lot of class about herself and she gave one decent massage and she seemed to like ole brother Walker.

Upon getting back to New Port, we started to talking about our night downtown and the girls. I admitted that I would like to see Ms. Chao again but I knew Lan, Jesus and Ms. Chao had total control of another meeting or not. I wondered how things would come off, all the way back to Long Bien Post, to change uniforms, and get my ass to work and try to keep my mind on work. I had wanted an encounter with one of these Vietnamese women and I was quite pleased with myself.

Upon reaching our billet, everybody seemed to have one of those how was it kind of looks on their faces. Stewart came up smiling and said, new guys no more man. You lost your cherries, meaning we had got laid. He followed that statement with "Which one did you have? "Huh?" "Which one?" As if he knew whom the girls might had been "Which one," he asked again. "Kim, Chao, Lee-Lin, Phan who?" I said "Chao," "Chao, he was laughing like a mad man. "No, not Chao." "Ronald gonna flip!" That Jesus! Wow, you had Chao! Unfucking real, Chao. "And who did Bro. Rochester get?" I replied, hunching my shoulders. I didn't even get her name. "Ask Bro. Rochester," I answered in kind of a shitty way. She ain't nothing but a trick, I was thinking, a no good hussy. Without knowing Stewart had knocked me down and kicked my butt with this little information like Jesus had at one time or another taken damn near everybody, everybody downtown to his crib to get a little play and those chicks were like the standard around the way party girls. And to add insult to injury, the one named Chao had given Ronald that hated black people and sure as hell didn't like me. Chao had burnt him! Yes, set him on fire! It took almost three weeks for Ronald to shake that case of the clap! He had to take double shots of penicillin and a lot of pills. Stewart told us Ronald's clap case was so bad he had to wear a rubber all day long and change them over and over because he was filling the rubbers up with pus just that quickly. Yea, she gave him a real good dose. This news put fear in me, now I had been burnt before, no problem, but filling up rubbers with pus, that's another thing all together. Man, I had to find Jesus and talk about this.

Bro. Rochester seeing the look on my face knew to come help me out, said "Walker, don't listen to that shit." "You are alright man, no sweat. You'll see." "Anyway, we can always go to see the doc you know." Like all I could think of was first time out and I get burnt! I was thinking all kinds of stuff, if I hadn't got with Chao, may be she didn't do me any harm. Why would she burn me, man I was thinking some wild stuff. I knew one thing for sure right now I was going to sick call to have myself checked out! No pus was going to be coming out of me all day long. Straight after signing in the desk log, I signed out, sick call I hollered at Bro. Rochester and off to the medics. To get to this medical building, one would have need of a permission slip signed and for good cause. And with me I would need the Full Bird to sign off on the slip and that would mean he would be all in my shit, but no matter. It had to be done, so I forged his signature on the slip and on the medics I went.

I got there, man oh man, there was many a GI on sick call there. Then as I looked about, I saw that there were two awaiting lines, one for noncommissioned officers, hey! That's me! So I lined up (but we were really sitting, not standing). The wait was short. I was called into this office. A tall brother in a doctor's coat spoke but then put his fist out as to give me some Dapt. Puzzled, I just looked but then began to slapping out the Long Bien Post Dapt. Man, I thought this is one cool doctor here. The brother then asked, "What can I do for you brother. I'm brother Bro. Gator Man." He didn't say doctor, he said brother. I looked at his name tag, then I looked for his rank. All this dude had on was a blue undershirt, ok, so no rank showing. Just a cool brother here, I thought. Him still waiting for me to answer what I'm there for, asked again. "Can I help you?" "Yes, you can. I think I have the clap or something." "Really," he said laughing on the side. "Please pull down your pants and shorts if you would." I did the, the guy got two think pieces of squared glass things, told me to grab my penis and squeeze it. I did and he tried to get something on the glass from me, doing all of that squeezing on my joint. Nothing came out. He looked at me and asked me, "Are you sure you have Gonorrhea brother?" We are going to have to do another test, Mr. Walker Jr, as he looked over his paperwork. "Lean over that table there."

Now, I had been through this before, but to get what results, what was he talking about. Watching Slim like a hawk, I half-ass leaned over the table, he greased up his gloves and rammed his finger up my rectum, but then he started to push down doing something, this shit hurt, but he assured me soon this will be over, over brother as some shiny, glassy, sticky syrup like stuff came out of me onto the thin piece of glass. "There!" he said with a raised voice. "There we are, he took the glass slide off to the side and started doing something. I wiped off, and fixed myself up and sat there waiting, about ten minutes passed. He came back over and said "You don't have any disease Brother Walker. None whatsoever."

I felt so relieved without thinking, I reached into my upper shirt pocket and pulled out a cigarette, not any cigarette but a rolled jay of reefer and I lit it up. The fellow was over at his desk filling out my return sick call slip and he seemed to take a deep breath in to sniff the aroma of the Herb. I scoped this and I held the joint out as to offer him a drag. Surprisingly enough, he took the joint and hit it like a champ. He hit again and then took a shorty shot. We both laughed as he took the shorty blast. The door opened, in stepped a young Spec 4 blue shirted tee. "Bill, ole Bill, how can I help you my new friend," asked with a giggle in his voice. "Ain't you finished with him yet? "Nope, may be in about 3 more of these blasts," The still nameless attendant answered. Bro. Gator Man you have a room full of people waiting to see you man. Bro. Gator Man straightened up for a moment, then said "Sir you are free to live another day, be black and proud" and stepped away. I gathered myself together and stumped the now roach I held. Bro. Gator Man walked over to a Bunsen burner and lit the flame. The gas from the Bunsen burner and the Herb made for an exotic aroma smelling air freshener. I bid farewell and left the aid station.

On my way back to my Company, I was thinking, how I didn't still know anything about Nam. I didn't know the people, the language, customs and if to be here, I would have to learn all I could about Monson coming up, meaning it would be raining everyday, no traveling around in that rain, stuck in the Company. I would have the housekeepers close, so I can learn a lot from them, and may be do the both of them. I could find out all about these creeps I was working with and I could find out where this Post came together and begin to make some money and I could start to study how to speak Vietnamese like a native (yea) this is going to be my new plan, this could work.

Now, about the chick, well she would find another boyfriend after I don't show up for seconds. I didn't owe her anything. She did all of the Company anyway. Let Jesus find a replacement GI for her. Yes, I had made up my mind that's how I was going to handle that. Things were going on at work that had the office buzzing. A place called Bearcat was catching hell. Bearcat was just south of Saigon City. It had firebases, where artillery was shot long distances to keep the enemy at bay and the Cong had made a push to overrun that area. Support was needed, and that meant we had to get to work, making sure they got supplied, it took bullets and bombs, missiles to get that done, that's us and in between the melee it took us to clean up (blow up) any down helicopters, tanks, ammo depots and supplies that got damaged.

    Now, Bro. Rochester nor me had been sent on a mission yet and we would probably be the last ones to be called upon to go, but we would at least get the experience of the mission's contingency and how it worked, an on the job experience type thing. The enemy was trying to sneak in under the cover of rain I overheard someone say. No way! In working on this mission, I learned how this war went. All of this Army stuff was real complex and if it all came together, it worked like a charm but if only one thing went whacked, all hell would break loose. The little things like rain could mean the difference if the Company was won or lost and that means just the battle that was fought, not the entire war effort but men's lives were at risk and that was serious, our GIs.

    Everyone was showing off what skills they had. We were working as a unit of one. The orders for munitions were working well. The boys in the field were catching it. We were told and we could not fumble the ball. Bearcat was important to us. It always told how things to come off in the South would go. If Bearcat went bad, the other firebases would surely suffer for it was on the outskirts. The reports on what was going on were keeping the phones and printer running. The push from the South was stopped by the U.S. and its allies. The word was that a great body count was taken in the five days but we prevailed. The office was celebrating how we had handled our part, but now the interesting portion was upcoming.

There was to be a couple of kits chosen to gather information, confirm expenditures, check supply level and most of all destroy any damaged goods that stood inoperable on the grounds, which meant blow it up or blow it down or blow it all around. EOD (Explosive Ordnance), the job the new guys stood a chance in hell of going on the temporary duty, but one always hoped to be chosen for the OJT (on job training), just to have it under his belt.

When assignments were given out, Bro. Rochester and me along with two others were to go on a tour of local ammo depots in the area of Long Bien to include a small village, Bien Hoa with our task ahead of us, I made ready to take it on. Now, I was one of headquarters boys coming down off the hill going into the field groups of which the hill people seldom did and when so, they were viewed as safely kept, book learned, stiff assholes. They most times didn't know how to gel with the common GIs but I just wanted to see the look on the faces of those guys when they saw me and ole Bro. Rochester leading the bunch and to having a lot of them reporting and taking orders from young Blacks, Oh boy, bring it on!

Two days after all suited up with files and calculators and field phones, MP escort and a small fleet of trucks, we were off, on our way to the outer perimeter of this giant Post. Unit after unit gates upon gates we went through, towers, bunkers and bunker lines on forever coming up on a small camp. Our convoy pulled in. We stepped down, a orderly room clerk greeted us, directed us to the First Sergeant and a couple of other E-fives and an E-sixes. We cut the yang yang down to a minimum and off to the sites. On the way we hit the ammo slits, huge dirt burns, separated each with its own posted signs, fire extinguishers, perfectly cleared of all obstacles. This place had all of the makings of a textbook example of what a depot should be. It all came together here. There was also a heliport that a group of riggers worked 24 hours a day shifts on site to receive any sort of ammo sent over from Long Bien Depot.

We had to check on site quantities, record counts and evaluate conditions of storage and get a true count of small arms, munitions and motor counts. Now this was suppose to be an easy job, but always some things come up, like just when we thought this was going to be easy, we discovered lot after lot of ammo that was to be sent back to the U.S. almost a year ago and on top of that canisters that were to be also still on the grounds. These items were almost hidden away but we stumbled upon them. What was supposed to be an unused burn area off by itself in a swamp like area, unkempt, overgrown but recent tractor tracks and rough terrain forklifts had gone through recently.

Well, we checked it out and found the dirty deed and we put the entire Camp to work, cleaning the joint. When we came into the Camp we were hardly noticed, but now the entire Camp knew about the hill boys and they didn't care for us one bit. Well, we had a job to do and we did it. Now, I never liked to be stood over as I worked, but the guys had to be overridden by us because we didn't know what else might had been buried in this dump and we did find infraction to the codes. This spot was a graveyard! A real death house of wares without knowing we had stumbled upon one of the large cases of dumped live ammo left over from the late 60's. Bien Hoa was a hotbed for the bad guys back then, men still got killed over here nightly and this area was off limits to Americans, yet within arms reach of the largest Post in South Viet Nam. Years before big scale battles had gone on to take this area and tons upon tons of munitions were stored here. This was all news to us but we were learning. In uncovering its secrets, we found every kind of ammunition known to kill a man buried on the grounds.

Just outside of the new standing ammo depot extra rough terrain forklifts, trucks and almost every man from our outfit was called upon to get involved. Well, nothing or no credit was given to Bro. Rochester and me for being so sharp and the anger about us putting all of those men to work blew over. Most were glad for they had been working all around and over this junk and could have gotten killed by an accident of weight of one of their tracts or forklift or a black powder explosion to set the entire place up and I'll explain about the powder factor later, its bad stuff. I might as well explain now.

Black powder or gunpowder is risky stuff. One spark can set it off. In some cases we had to put wooden soles on our feet, or rubber soles so it would be spark free. black powder also even when it gets wet, it is still black powder and dried out it reverts back to it's deadly self, ready for action to blow. No one at the Camp wanted to set off any dry left over black powder region. The site took on a lot of manpower but it got cleared by headquarters. A job well done. This went down good for our kit of four. We were ordered into the office of the Full Bird. All were there, we got mentioned and for Bro. Rochester and me, we were true members of the club and now we would go out on TDY (temporary duty assignment) assignments. The brothers had shown there worth for all to know. We did it.

The rains came right on time. Life was really different, but with a purpose for me. I spent more and more time asking and speaking Vietnamese. I was getting really good. I was studying from Bro. Rochester's cassette tape player and trying to teach him a little. The housekeepers were really into having someone who could converse with them. The conversations got better and better. I started to ask about relationships, religion and about how they felt about us being here in Nam. All they cared about was they had jobs and they were getting paid, nothing else mattered. I also found out they did like whoring, but it was money once again, no love was in it, just money. Kim stated it only took "tee-tee" time anyhow. The more I got to know these women and others that worked for us GIs, I found that these ladies knew how to handle us young men and knew just what they were doing to survive in this man's war.

The extra smart ones catered in another way. They were mules, they bought in dope everyday. Some were on their own as transporters, but some really had it going on with GIs acting as sponsors, giving them big money to act as suppliers. They had routes, and other housekeepers that formed a chain of dealers in some units and to think I could understand what they were saying. I would walk about listening to all of the different conversations unnoticed for GIs didn't have the sense nor the time to learn their language. They thought anything could be said aloud with no consequence of their actions. There were plenty cases of theft and the discussions were never carried on in English and almost always the GIs lost out on everything. I heard a lot and knew plenty of secrets. I even capitalized on knowing Vietnamese. I found out about how and when a stash of drugs was being delivered to the Post and I ripped them off in the name of all the GIs that had gotten ripped off and got no justice. Plus I could understand any and all of the discussions on who the women liked and I certainly cashed in on that. Yes, the rainy season and being trapped on Post proved to be a trip.

Things at work had almost come to a halt. The rains prevented the helicopter from flying. The battles slowed down. We mostly sat around the office doing nothing. When we had a big meeting to be held in Saigon at the MACV (Military Assistance Command Viet Nam) Headquarters the HQ that supported Saigon City and the Air Force was there for both civilian and Armed Forces. All of us were up for that. The move didn't take long. Our unit was housed on Plantation Road the very top of the red light section of Saigon. A mile and a half long strip that had bars on both sides of the road for as far as the eye could see. This road had a black top asphalt made for all of the traffic of the trucks that traveled the road 24 hours a day, a main supply route and this road was the playground for all of the servicemen of all of the Armed Forces fighting in South Viet Nam.

      Speckled in between the bars were little stores that sold everything sold on the black market. Name it, you could find it here from the beginning of Plantation Road, to the end the valued sales items were women, young pretty girls. As a rule most dates had a going rate of $4.00 American or $72.00 Viet Nam Piasters. For $20.00 U.S.A. dollars we had $50,000 Piasters. Yes, we were considered boss rich! With most GIs being 18 years old, away from home, and ready for plenty of loving, we took cold advantage of the situation of getting laid! The Army knew what was going on. The Army would have the women tested for sexually transmitted diseases, whorehouses on this strip were protected by MPs, CID, and the Vietnamese police of which the GIs called the white mice.

      These police were feared by the Vietnamese police. They would kick those peoples brains out of their heads if caught doing something wrong or unlawful. They would beat them right out in the open, really. They could be seen collecting bribes from shopkeepers and the independent whores, the thugs called the cowboys. They collected also from the taxi drivers, bus drivers, also. Yes, Saigon City was a city for real. It was going to be one trip down here in Ole Saigon City and Bro. Rochester and I and my unit were to be up front to take it all in. We found out in our new quarters we were not going to stay together. Some of us were working in different areas of MACV Headquarters, but we all slept in the bays in the building.

      Bro. Rochester went to work in Requisitions and I worked in the Retrograde Section, or he ordered supplies like weapons, bullets, bombs, missiles, grenades. I was in charge of getting receipt of the spent shell casings, misfired, damaged and hazardous materials for disposal.

Chapter 9
Specialized Training

Now, I was getting to do what they had trained me for, disposal and I thought I was going to blow one or two of the steps to get to do disposal work EOD. But I was wrong again. First you learn, then you practice, then you learn some more, then may be you get to practice with a journeyman, I was told by a Senior Sergeant, so practice!

This new Post took some getting use to. At Long Bien Post, the 82 Ord. Ammo/EOD Supply Unit was elite! The top of the hill boys, the "Can do Bunch". We were treated special but we were second betty here. We had to abide by Long Bien Post rules, like Saigon Army and Air Force men could wear civilian clothes after work, they seemed to work only 8 hour shifts. They could leave work, clean up, change clothes, go downtown, party until 11:30 p.m. and then back to Post or stay downtown until they had to return to work.

A lot of the Air Force guys lived downtown or off Post period. We had to always wear our OD green uniforms and our caps on our heads. We had to carry ID cards, and our Army patches were different from MACV patches as if we answered to a lower God or something, but all in all I was glad to be there. It was in Saigon City! Once real work started, I found that this place was real strict! Like MPs standing in the hallways, officers all over the place, office after office of Vietnamese women working as clerks. Most of military personnel were in charge of hundreds of Vietnamese clerks and aides or the entire office had only U.S. personnel and was off limits to all others. We had to be classified. We carried top secret clearances so we went all over and were assigned travel orders, passes for the most part. We are treated well, respected and we get along well with our fellow workers but problems come up at lunch times.

These guys seem to have problems with Long Bien men trying to take over certain job tasks and running them our way, but we find a way to meet in the middle. In most cases, I must admit the unit of the disposal unit seemed to have more experience than what we had, only because they had the prime task of protecting Saigon and having 15 firebases to cover weekly and they stayed on the move. They had a constant turn over of men coming and going back home, that we didn't. Most of our guys had 2 or more tours which made us as good as them. We were tenacious (hang tough guys) and we jelled well with MACV men. I worked under a Captain down here, young but smart. He was from Ohio. He kept a Captain enlisted man relationship with me and that was alright with me because I knew my job. We had about 20 or so clerks.

One was Ms. Mai Lee, a fine Vietnamese woman, long black hair, dark brown yes and a cute little nose, with a black girl walk. Mai Lee walked the Unit like a jail guard and the women worked like ants in an ant hill, heads always down, typing and working nonstop. All were dressed in pretty long native dresses with sandals only lifting their heads to smile, then back to work. I leave my office space to go to the water cooler often just to look at all of these pretty women, down one way, up the other way trying to take a look at the them all. I would hear whispers from time to time as I would walk by. Not one of them knew I could understand what they were saying and I wouldn't let on that I did, but one day as I walked about I heard Mai Lee say he is kind of Dapp-Why (cute/beautiful) and I knew I would get her and I did. I found out she had lived with a white Officer. Months before, he had returned to the USA, he had left her very rich. She had bought a house in one of the better parts of Saigon City, no kids, but kind of old as far as Vietnamese girls went. She was 25 years old, but still looked good. Most Vietnamese women start to break at age 25 years old and get to looking old fast after that for some reason, but since she was not a working girl (she had gone through less wear and tear) plus she had been to school, college and had this fine job. And the house looked like a Hollywood dream building with a large garden and fountain and ferns and palm trees and flowers. It was boss and now it had me.

Now, Mai Lee knew I didn't have the rank the Captain had, nor the pay, nor that I was going to stay in Saigon City but I guess she liked me too much. For she allowed me in over and over again and kept on loving me down. But no woman on the job would look my way once I got hooked up with Mai Lee, not one. I allowed her to know I spoke Vietnamese and she made sure I learned to speak it well and was trying to teach me to read and write it. But kept me clued in to keeping it a secret to protect myself while in this city, reminding me that all (didn't love nor like the GI) Mai Lee taught me that there were men and women that hated the GIs, both black and white s.

Other women felt sorry for the Blacks, because they had learned of us as slaves of the white man and felt we were forced into this way by the draft and knew we would be slaves once we returned back to America. Others felt we kill their people so we were the same as the white soldiers. But all of them hated the way Vietnamese women and girls were treated by the GIs! I often thought how did the white Captain treat her when he had her, and however I was going to treat her as if she were my wife and love here and do right by her no matter when I was to return to Long Bien Post. Mai Lee not only took me all over Saigon City, introduced me to many friends, relatives of hers, but allowed me to really get to know her. I saw pictures of grandparents, aunts, uncles and their children and their children. I ate at their houses, we visited the zoo, went to the Asian movies. I was really into this woman and it didn't cost me one cent. Now, we ate well. I was getting plenty of food from one of my buddies. He was a mess cook, E-6 James Cash from Philly, PA, cool cat. He had a pretty Chinese girl named Lynn or Ms. Lynn I called her, pretty. She lived in Cho-Lon, the Chinese part of Saigon. They were really strict. I didn't know how he pulled her, but he did. He was a 20 year man (a lifer) and 30 something years old. He supplied me with chicken, pork, lamb, ham and all of the veggies the Army had, not to mention sweets, and USA sugar! Worth it's weight in gold in Viet Nam, American sugar, not brown sugar but white sugar (yes) sold real well! On the black market! And he and I made a pretty dollar on it. Mai Lee sold at least a ton or two of it (no lie) by the 100 lb bag. Coffee was also a good seller. By not having to pay for sex, room and board, I got to send my money home to help my people out and I did. Mai Lee every now and again would talk about having a baby but never about taking her back to the USA. She is going on 26 years old in her country and being with an American, she wouldn't probably ever get married, nor be courted by a Vietnamese man of honor and have a baby. I did as I had always done smoked dope, but she never once said one thing about it. But some nights when I was really tore up she would sure then try to drain my body for all of the sperm I had in me, as if knowing the Heroin would keep me going. She would wear me out!

Now, time marches on. Back on the job, a report of some shipment of shell cases being buried at a defunct firebase back in 1969 were to be dug up and to be shipped back to the USA. These shell casings were brass and worth a pretty penny. A kit of 3 men were to go to the site to record, inspect and set up the shipment (now that was in my ball park) and I was going to be called up for the tour. I was up for the event. I took a lot from the guys about going into the field and life in the bush and Viet Cong and sappers (suicide bombers) and snipers and stuff but they all wished me well. Mai Lee didn't say one thing. She just gave me long stares and mumbled Walker, Walker time and time again. Without a lot of talking, Mai Lee knew something I didn't. She had men in her life before me, she had lived with, loved other men who had been affected by the war, the field and knew I would come back changed and she was oh so right.

    First, we had a briefing meeting. We were told not to leave the Post after having the meeting. Also not to discuss our mission to any one and no one was to mean nobody! We were to stay together as a group. We got our gear gathered together, and waited, and waited. Then we saddled up, a short ride on a helicopter passing numerous little camps, until we saw there was nothing but jungle, but then there was miles and miles of roads, asphalt roads, trucks after trucks, then trailers upon trailers for miles, buildings looking like they belonged in a major city. There were little parks, roadways and fences. These things were unreal! They were out here in the middle of nowhere, soldiers on guard, Posts and jeeps and helicopters lined up in formation. The same as in the rear, no one had told us to expect this!

    We had landed. Trucks awaited us, Philly pads were across this huge field and to the left were ammo burns, quite a few of them. Later we found out tons of ammo was stored there and it seemed to be steadily coming in to this place. We stayed there that night. There were a lot of civilians in this spot and a lot of officers. All young officers. This place was a carbon copy of Tan Son Nhut. It had everything, the buildings, all of them had air conditioners. It seemed everyone had a Jeep. They even had a nighttime mess hall. Most of the officers had insignias I had never seen and they sure as hell, not a one said anything to us. We stayed close to our sleeping quarters after dust. The next morning about 4:30 a.m. onto the trucks and we drove on and on. Two Jeeps at the head of the convoy loaded with M-60 gunners and two young soldiers in the front, about 10-12 trucks, then a Jeep to the rear. He was equipped the same as the other Jeeps. We were flying down those dirt roads. Every now and again, we could see a Cobra gun ship following us. That always made you feel extra safe. In passing, we saw plenty of people walking on both sides of the road. We saw fields with water buffalos and I guess it was rice they were working but the dust was being kicked up so badly, you had to look hard to see all of the sights. We even saw some of our boys looking worn, these boys were field tested, real GIs. I thought about this for a long while. This ride was just beginning to take its toll.

Hours later, we heard our driver yell "Fire base, yahoo." Bro. Rochester and I both hung out the back of the truck holding on to the tarp almost swinging in the wind. There was this huge beehive looking thing way up on this mountain looking hill. Once again out in the middle of nothing. Not a tree around for about a mile. It looked like you could see all the way back to Saigon City. There were four sets of fences, all razor wire and tower Posts and huge breaks in between each fence. Then another set of fences and towers and a huge break on and on fence and razor wire and breaks. Then bunkers and more razor wire for miles. It went all around the mountainside for as far as I could see. It was something to behold. Wow! I thought, what a place! My thoughts were interrupted by a jolt of the truck shifting gears.

We had come to a huge ramp. The ramp was on a huge incline straight upwards. And I mean upwards. Man, the driver was punching gears from low range to high range, then back to low gears again, winding the gears again and again. When we hit the top of the incline, we jumped across that gate opening and it seemed like we were in a race car. The truck was wide open, but the brother could drive, boy could he drive. He had it under control and slowed us down to a stop. It didn't seem to affect any of the GIs on the base. I guess they were use to this going on.

We parked and met up with a first Sergeant and a couple of E-6s that looked like they had been in WWII. They started cracking right off about our pretty boots and uniforms to insult us off at the start but I thought, they don't know I'm from B-more. You don't (F) with me. If they wanted trouble, well! Come on with it! We followed them to their mess hall, a small table was full with enlisted men, all of them look bad. They were looking sleepless, just plain rough. The mess hall was the worse I had ever seen, broken tables, chairs, poor lighting, hot as hell in there, smoky, but who was I to judge.

Top Sergeant told us of our task, short and sweet. He told us to go with this GI to find our quarters and rest while we could. We didn't know what he meant, but we would soon find out and find out we did. This place was a trip. The entire mountain was a man made mountain of dirt, rocks, boulders, concrete mixture piled up. Some 10 stories or so. I mean up there, then topped off with huge storage containers, prefab buildings and platforms for the 105 mm, 155 mm guns to shoot them out at the enemies miles away. Deep bunkers dug into the top base plus another beehive dirt shape mound with hundreds of holes dug into it where us GIs slept and lived in. It was black and wild looking with walkways all around it in layer to the top. One could get lost in the maze inside of this big dirt pile. It had loud speakers all over and chatter stayed on the line. On this huge hill it seemed that the GI could hide themselves at will, with really nowhere to go, but they did. Bro. Rochester and I shared what was a very large room. It had holes in the walls where airlines were embedded, light extension lines filled the ceiling all through the tunnels to each compartment and at the end of some corridors were the heads (bathroom stools), the showers were outside in another building. Pretty much the quarters were the same as any other but the place was made of dirt, and plywood and junk, but it was cool. You did not feel the heat of the outside at all. Now at some periods of the day all hell broke loose.

Orders would come in for support to a group out in the deep field and all would spring into action. The entire beehive would be jumping. Everybody was working. Mr. White, as his name tag on Top Sergeants shirt label listed him would walk about like a big turkey. He knew he owned this spot. He wore earphones taking directions on his phone from someone in the field and his boys were working those guns. Two of his guys stood at the ammo rack, one passed a shell, 105 mm to the other. He shoved it in to the back of the huge gun, slammed the door, the top had this thing that looked like a protractor. He gagged it and slipped it on to a slit on top of the gun. It looked like a gun hammer. He stepped to the side, hollered first in the hole, the trapper pulled the wire line, then everybody covered their eyes, all except us dummies. We didn't, and my ears rang for three hours. The first time I witnessed this fire in the hole going on, I bet we got some earplugs ASAP.

After each firing, a trooper that had some kind of mittens, picked up the spent shells. Still smoking hot and threw it in a bin to his side and they geared up for another shot. Fire in the hole over and over and over again. This could go on for hours, I lie not! After a firing session, some of the guys just sat around holding their heads in their hands. Others were crying, some had blood leaking from their ears, eyes all reddish. These GIs were spent, but there work was not over. The gun crew had to clean these big guns, oil them, restock the ammo bins, clean up the spent shells and await to be cleared by the top. Not until then could they rest. Man, I thought what a hell of a job they had! Our job was support. Yes, we were there, but not to work like that. Our job was to count the live ammo, count spent ammo rounds, canisters, check on their storage of said rounds, write reports of any misfires of rounds, order sorties from the rear if needed to replace damaged rounds and check all of the rigging equipment on site and order new ones if needed and coordinate return spent shells by trucks or helicopter lifts. This trip was an eye opener experience in the least. But I was to take away more than I expected.

  After all of the firing, when things settled down, after darkness had set in and us GIs got together in the beehive, the talk was that most of the GIs hated this place, being stuck in the middle of nowhere, nowhere to go! Seeing the same things everyday for a year, the mail only coming when the helicopter dropped it off and hardly ever during the rainy season. No PX, no commissary stores, no women, bad radio reception and all night fire in the holes and they all had hearing problems and boss headaches all of the time.

  Sure they got a few days at Vung Tau R&R but back to the hive and hell all over again. A lot of the guys would go AWOL when they hit the rear or act like fools with all of that freedom and easy time and get into real shit over the girls back there. A few of the hive boys had overdosed trying out the Saigon dope and on the hive some had habits that I knew they had to catch hell getting a supply but the truck driver would bring the junk in to them but they paid five and ten dollars more than it cost back in Saigon. The reefer was outrageous because most of the GIs smoked "Jays" like crazy at the drop of a hat plus it was harder to hide on the trucks. The top Sergeants knew the men were getting off on junk but what could they do? They needed the manpower, plus what the hell was there to do out there but read comic books and dream of home, your girl and away from this place. The guys in the rear cried about being bored, but they could at least get around, walk about and bitch about things. These guys were locked up on a giant manmade hill of dirt! I thought a lot about the way they had to do their tour and I felt blessed but now I knew I had to get to go on more of these assignments to really find out what this war was about. We returned to Saigon, turned in the reports. Already talk was about going to Camrone Bay Depot and Phu Bia. I wanted in on both of the temporary assignments. Most of the guys in the outfit had gone to both of the camps before so they didn't care if another person went instead of themselves. Plus most of them were on their second tour of Viet Nam.

Meanwhile, we had to wait to see who was to go on the trip. While gone though only a short period of time from MACV new orders were cut. I was to go downtown more often to an Attachment Unit in the Embassy dispatching documents and stuff and checking their records. I found out Bro. Rochester as usual was again ordered too. This was big time, there was the elite, top brass, civilians and upper class Vietnamese working class. Right off I was glad to go down there. The clerk pool was huge, so of the best students of the college were working there. All of the women wore native clothes, long dresses, pretty bright colors, sandals, long black hair flowing. Their faces made up like dolls and they all spoke English, French and of course Vietnamese. But they had a silent code to try to keep to themselves until married. But all of them wanted to go to the USA. Believe me! That was their dream day in and day out, the USA. To promise one of them you would take them back with you, you owned their soul. But then to promise to take one of these women, you would take them back home with you could get you killed because that was serious! They would claim you, tell all Viet Nam you and she were one! You had better not mess around with another woman! They would get you killed or (crocodiled) killed for sure! And the people expected that to happen. If to tell a girl that and go back on your word, you had better stay on Post for your last month of your tour and still you had better watch your back because her people worked all over the open Post, such as Saigon, Long Bien, Hue' and about 40 other Posts across Viet Nam and us GIs loved to have our pictures taken and those pictures would be the death of us. They would use them and get the cowboys to take us out. You would never know what hit you. Dead, just dead, you would be and no one in Viet Nam would know who did it.

Anyhow, I was in seventh heaven, women wall to wall on my first day working there. I was dazzled by all of the pretty women. But this one, this one, man, she was all there was. She looked at me as to say who are you looking at huh? I don't now if it was with dislike, disgust, hatred or what? But she interested me. I saw her three times that same day and each time she looked at me the same, then disappeared like a ghost. During lunch break I even had the look out for her. She was nowhere to be seen. The fourth day in she appeared again. She hung her head down low, like one of the old women of the country, and walked semi-side way as we passed one another in the hallway. I was going to get to know this woman, even if she didn't want to know me! Each time I had an encounter with this woman, the more I wanted to know her. My interest was showing too at Mai Lee's. She had felt something and it wasn't that I had taken the trip to Bear Cat Fire Base. Mai Lee asked me straight questions about how I liked the job at the Embassy and the girls there she asked me if I butterfly on her. As to say from flower to flower like a butterfly. "You don't love me anymore Walker?" "You no love?" "Soon you leave Mai Lee Walker, you leave me Walker?" I would never answer. Love was too deep for me to understand. How could I answer? The pressure was so tough that I started going to the Red Light section of town again to try to gain my single GI standing again.

Going into a sunglass store, just a block outside of the front gate of Tan Son Nhut I saw Brother Gator Man, the medic from Long Bien Post. He was buying sunglasses also. We greeted, dapped and told of how long since we had seen one another. Bro. Gator Man told me he had a girlfriend in Saigon and she had a house and worked at one of the PX's. His friend was named Lon, and she had a sister. Well, I was trying to find my wild side again and he was talking about me getting hooked up again so I turned down the offer to meet his girl's sister. So, we went to one of the smoke houses. The house was as most of smoke houses were, but blocks from the Post. The place was full with loose women of all ages, plenty of drugs, food, and some had newspapers from the USA. If no drugs were on hand one of the girls or some young boys was on hand to act as a runner. But the house made its money by use of it's upstairs. The sex room and they got plenty of use. These houses gave us an outlet to the entire neighborhood, all of its women, their daughters and if you wanted granddaughters, but Blacks had a code. No little girls, no "Cherry Girls" (virgins). That was a no! no! No raping little girls, too many women to choose from and we would choose and choose over and over again for as little as $5.00 for all day long. Bro. Gator Man and I wind up teaming up a lot. He liked staying stoned and again I was "off to the races." Still working, still waiting for the assignments to hit the duty board, staying stoned 24-7. I started to loose weight. Mai Lee was worried, she talked some nights all night about me getting (crazy) smoking (con sai) dope, but she still crawled up under me each night. I was getting wilder and wilder. I started going into the restricted quarters of 267, one of the bad sections of True Mon Key, where all of the native people lived, way off the main stretch where GIs walked safely with no fear of getting beat up, robbed or even killed.

  Bro. Gator Man had introduced me to the back streets, his girlfriend lived there and we walked it like we were in Portsmouth, VA where Bro. Gator Man came from or Baltimore, MD, where I came from with no fear of anything or anyone. The people had to think we were cowboys for sure, looking for trouble. But we were just stoned out of our minds, single minded on going where we were going and doing whatever what some people Viet Nam said we were (Dinky Darr) crazy! Bro. Gator Man had a slick uniform, a blue, sleeveless, v-neck square bottom shirt with a red cross on it. He wore no stripes on it and he wore airborne jump boots, but he had the screaming eagle insignia on his cap. He was 101st Airborne, but detached at Long Bien Post Medical Evac. He was a buck Sergeant (three strips) Infantry Medic field status, but he was also strung on dope, and women and adventures. To keep me from getting busted by Headquarters MACV for being in the off limits areas, we decided to disguise me. So, I started to be a Medic also. All I had to do was to change shirts. I found out this little change had its reward. Oh, did it have its rewards. See, medics were the same as doctors! They healed the sick, cured the clap (STD), had medicines for all kinds of stuff and everybody in Viet Nam liked the doctors of the USA. Every mama, son, madame in the country wants a medic as a friend. But I found out the cowboys like the medic also, like to stick them up for penicillin, Amitriptyline, the new wonder drug used to knock the clap out in a few days.

  So, we started to carrying 45 caliber guns. Now, just imagine the two of us, blown away, higher than a kite, armed down looking for trouble in the off limits parts of the city in the middle of the war! Yes, we were for sure (Dinky Darr) crazy! We would be out there way after 11:00 p.m. when we were to be back on Post and Bro. Gator Man was suppose to be back at Long Bien Post, 30 miles away. No, he was in Saigon City until 4:30 a.m., then to New Port to catch the bus back to Long Bien Post. But he stayed downtown every night with Lon. Me, I was catching hell from Mai Lee. Now, soon I knew we would be friends no more for sure and as I knew we said goodbye or Chow Mai Lee, Chow Walker and I walked away. Now, I still saw her at MACV, we slept together for a time, but soon she had another GI, a older fellow, but Mai Lee said he was nice to her, he treated her good and that sat well with me. So, I backed off. Then one day, I just went on my lunch break and I had found me this quiet little place to light up a "Jay". I lit it up, pulled up on the smoke, when a voice said, "Kill yourself and cheat the Viet Cong, huh?" I almost choked when I saw that girl. The one I had been looking for, the ghost, she was right here. She crept up on me doing wrong. Ah man, I have messed up. I have blew, my introduction to move in. My thoughts were running all over the place. She spoke again. "You go into 267 like you own Viet Nam." "You wear two Army patches, you sleep with too many girls and you try to kill yourself because of shame". "Yes, Mein Dan you (Dinky Darr) boo-coo dinky darr, real crazy". Then she walked away again, again she was gone. Later that day I told Bro Gator Man and Rochester about how I got caught by the ghost, as I now called her. Rochester said she must have cared or she would not have said anything. And she had been watching me or had heard about me and wanted to let me know she knew or cared. Now, I had to talk to her, I had to! First I had to clean myself up. Now I was serious about getting clean again and Mia Lee out of my system. Bro. Gator Man had me acting crazy as hell, the smoke houses were killing me slowly. I was thin, sleepy all of the time and I seem to be getting into stuff that didn't make any sense. Plus this woman was refine, good looking and more my age and had a good job. I made sure she saw my progress but I didn't know then. She also saw me after work. She lived in 267, the off limits area I hung out in (where the people lived) where I really acted like a wild man. Most of the GIs that crossed the lines of the off limits area, were either crazy, head deserters, or AWOLers, bad GIs and Bro. Gator Man and I walked that area as if we lived there. In times past Bro. Gator Man and myself had committed crimes and did plenty of terrible deeds in 267 and a lot of the folks just knew we were "dinky darr" (crazy).

    I was steadily thinking just how much this girl had seen or heard of my going on. But I was going to show her my good side. I sure needed a change. I started to creep pass the large gated room she worked in, sometimes 4 or 5 times a day. Then by chance I was on the 3rd floor of the Embassy Xeroxing some papers and she came in to the room. We first just looked at one another, nothing was said. I broke the silence with a little of my Vietnamese, "Chow Min Joy Co (good morning Ms.)." She looked surprised and smiled. She lowered her head and said "Hello, Walker". "Walker!" She knew my name, even though it was printed on my shirt. I felt I was in! We just stood there. I offered the machine to her, she smiled and started to copy her stack of papers. I talked to her all through the process. She finished her copies and turned to walk out. I stated "I would like to see you again." She nodded up and down to answer yes. I asked where? She replied "Somewhere Viet Nam" and walked out of the room. Now, I didn't know what that meant but it was up for the rest of the day. But that bubble got busted, I had to extend my workday and order for ammo was needed at one of the firebases and that was my job. So, I stayed over. Bro. Gator Man was at the smoke house when I got there. He was kind of distant now, I had really shut down on my smoking so I wasn't acting the same as before, but he was still my boy. The guys were getting high and things and I wasn't, so I slide out. I was just walking and wasting time when I saw two young girls laughing and pointing at me. In the door of the house they were standing at was the woman…Man! There she was! I had passed this house time and time again and she lived here. Now, I knew she saw me and that I was seeing her, but I could not confront her. It was against her law. She would be shunned by her people for such an encounter in public. People would talk and call her a whore girl. I gave a nod and a smile and moved on slowly. I took a peek back and she was still watching me walk on down the cobbles lane street. I knew where she lived so that's what she meant somewhere Viet Nam, along the streets I was known to travel.

Now down this same street to its end was a street market. Everybody shopped there on the weekends, people upon people, talking, buying fruits and veggies and stuff and GIs and the people jelled there with no problems so that's where we would meet I thought, yes! There! As I planned, we started to meet there the first time. I didn't even know who she was. She had on a pointed straw hat, black pajamas, sandals, carrying a big basket. This outfit was quite different from her work clothes, but very becoming. Along with her were the same two young girls that had been pointing at me. We shopped side by side. She even steered me from some vendors that she considered to be shady. I had a good little shopping trip. The basket half filled. They left and walked back up the block and I slow walked behind the trio. Now, I had put almost a month into courting this girl and I had not even asked her name, so I did. I stopped her in the hallway on my visit to Headquarters' office at the Embassy. Her name was Phen Thi Hue and she was Cambocheea, Cambodian, not a Vietnamese. I had noticed she was darker, thicker and her eyes were more of a round shape but I had thought one of the brothers may have got next to her mother back in yesteryear, like black men had left their mark in Viet Nam, and the whole world so why not a little same, same me in her, I thought. But I was happy to hear Thai or Cambodian. That meant black babies could come out of a union with a girl like this.

The more I saw of this girl, the more I liked her. I spent every day now at the lunch garden in her company even though there were about sixty more women and I don't know how many officers all around. Only one guy always seemed to interrupt every time for some lame reason to call Hue' back to work. Oh yea, overseas, one is addressed by their last name. But about that chump I didn't like him from the first meeting. The first encounter with this guy. Now he was a major, an officer, and he knew it! He also flaunted it and he had a thing for Ms. Hue'. Yes, he did. He had and was Viet Nam love sick for Ms. Hue'! And she didn't like him. Come to find out he had offered to marry her and take her back to the USA. He had sent gifts, money, had run off other young guys whom had taken a slight interest in Ms. Hue' and now comes along me! A lowly Speck 5 Sergeant. That fool had no idea that I had dried out, slacked up on the black market sells, and just stopped having a hell of a time, trying to pull that girl and I just found out she was Cambodian! Hell no! He wasn't running me anywhere. Also, the woman dug me. She liked Walker too much for sure, com sai. I took a lot of pride every time I ran into that sucker in the hallways. Most times he would stop and look at me real crazy like. But he would get back. Every time Hue' and I was talking, he would interrupt with work issues. But for sure, he wasn't coming downtown around 267 Tru-Minn Kie and Soul alleyway (for sure!) Not down, that would be an adventure! Hue' and I were really getting close. I saw her mother from time to time and she had seen how her daughter reacted when she saw me, but said nothing even at the open market. She just watched me like a hawk! Then one afternoon as I walked on purpose past her house, Mama Son waved for me to come see, come see. I couldn't believe this. Now, anyone could talk to a Mama Son anywhere, at any time, but she called to me to come see, come see. So, I walked over. She said in pretty good English, "Soul you love Phen Thia Hue, Soul? I didn't know what to say, nor did I want to say I loved Hue'. I'd be washed up, locked in! I said I loved anyone in Viet Nam or the USA loved man! That was heavy! Liked yes, wanted yes, lusted (for sure) but loved! I just smiled and then started to talk in Vietnamese. I told my name, my rank, pointing to my stripes, told her where I worked, told her I liked Viet Nam. After all of that, she just laughed, turned half face, started walking back towards her door and said "Walker love Phen Thia Hue too much, Walker love sick Ms. Hue." I stood there sweating and wordless.

Later, as I told Bro. Rochester and Bro. Gator Man about the old woman, they red assed me about being in love and acting already like a married man of which I denied over and over. Now my buddies knew I had slacked up off the strip and thought I needed some street play. So, we went out that night. We hit Plantation Road and the bars. Man, I didn't know I missed the circuit so much. Within a half an hour, I was the ole me all over, wide open, but not as wild. I tricked with a couple of girls and smoked quite a few jays. I had a real good time (no lie). I stayed on Plantation Road that night at one of the whorehouses, cost me $10.00 in their money (pretty cheap). I got up at 4:00 a.m., my uniform was washed, pressed, boots shined, cost me one buck. Strange, it seemed not to carry the same weight. It seemed to carry a feeling like I had done something great, like I had worn the hooker out. I had conquered the mountain or king for a day. I thought real hard on that as I showered the sweat off the both of us down the drain. I thought, what am I going through? I told Bro. Rochester about my weird thinking, he just said I should ease up on smoking that shit and that was that.

Now with all of the people around 267 calling me Hue's boyfriend and her mother acting like I was a family member or something, things were getting too settled for me. I, single, young and there are a million young girls all around me and I am going to feel like a husband! But I dig this girl. Meanwhile, the Major was looking around in the background and Pandora's box was about to be opened on my lovesick ass. I received orders to return back up to Long Bien Post when I'm on temp duty to MACV Headquarters. Something was up, I knew it! Come to find out I was right. One of the new guys untrained, new in the country was to start tasks he didn't know a thing about. So, like a good GI, orders were orders. I packed up my grip and shipped out. I had my long goodbye with the fellows and loaded into the two ton. Now, I put on the long face for the staff at the office, knowing good and well I would be back on the six o'clock bus to Saigon and Tru Minn Kie Street at Plantation Road for sure! I had not made any plans on telling Hue' or her mother that I had been sacked. They would be kept in the dark for a couple of days or so. But, I had told Bro. Rochester all about the move. But unknowingly he had told Bro. Gator Man and Bro. Gator Man had talked to his girlfriend, Ms. Lon and she had said I could move in with them at her place. She had a spare room I could rent, so I was on. Man, all things were working out for me with no sweat. No sooner had I checked into Long Bien Post, I was ready to check back out.

But, first I had to reinstate myself back into the barracks on Post, because there were a few new guys that had come into the Company. One of the NGs (new guys) was this crazy lanky white guy that was working at my old desk spot in the room with Mr. Gross and Mr. Warren and Major Douglas. The cool Officer in charge (my man) the new guy was a know it all. Just off the boat, he knew more about everything than us Vets and to top it off, he hated Gooks. Gooks this and Gooks that, every other word. The other two new guys were low key but seemed to be jelling into Nam as any new person would seem to do. I didn't like this loud mouth punk (from wherever he came from) right off and I knew we would clash plus he had my old spot of which I was going to get back (for sure). The tension was thick. The first week back, I moved the desk I was assigned straight up to border his desk. I got an extension long phone cord and plugged it into the double socket with his and just leaned back in that chair and stared at that fool hours upon hours, never saying a word and doing less work. For, I had the rank and time in the country. Often the fool would try to fish information from me about where I would disappear during the nights only to show up in time for formation in the morning or try to talk about a people he didn't know a thing about but hated so much, but had his Tongue hanging out every time he would see a pretty young Vietnamese woman walk down the hall. And most of all I thought he had my old desk and my old spot and didn't deserve it (no way). He had to go. Also, my desk had a perfect eyeshot of the hallway where all of the clerks that worked in the big clerical pool with wall to wall women. So, I put up with it for as long as I could stand it, then I just switched my files and chair to my old desk and backed my gear up against the wall and reclaimed it as home again. Now, if there was a noise about the move, I didn't hear anything about it. Things just rolled along like nothing had ever happened and all of the questions stopped.

  Meanwhile, I paid my wash and iron dues to my housewives as usual and in many ways I was glad to see them again; for, Ms. Lon had taught me how to talk Vietnamese and had taught me almost all I knew about the country and I always wanted to get into Ms. Kim's pajama's anyway. Plus, we had history together. But they knew my heart belonged to Saigon City and its people. Thus, each evening they would pull the dust cover up on my empty bunk as if I had slept in it that night. I had a place to sleep, thanks to Ms. Lon and Bro. Gator Man, way up off of the Plantation Road, and I do mean way up there, not too many GIs dare venture up this way. Nothing but the people stayed up there or here. No cabs went up over town, just cyclos, the bucket hooded motorcycle hacks. The people's cabs, 25 pee and 50 pee anywhere in the city for the people, 100 pee for GIs from the gates of Tan Son Nhut up the way, was about 10 minutes hard driving and three times as hard a ride.

The streets were unpaved, dark, gang filled, cowboys and to be told Viet Cong. The first night up over town way, Bro. Gator Man gave me a .45 caliber gun and sling holster and said wear it on the outside of your shirt. Don't hide it Walker, you hear! Forewarned is to be forearmed. So, now I carried iron and two clips. We traveled together up here always. "Now say these two words Walker" (heard you) and I said ("heard you") and believe me we had nights I was glad I listened to those words. Ms. Lon, Bro. Gator Man's woman was a looker, half Chinese and half Vietnamese, thick-ankled, raven black hair, with cat shaped eyes, with a copper tone to her skin. She was pretty and spoke both languages, plus English in a singing voice style. Ms. Lon had a sister, Ms. Lana, pregnant by a white GI that had gone home to the USA that she still loved too much. Also, Ms. Lon, mom and poppy san were living. Her father was a barber and a half crazy brother that had just got drafted into the South Viet Nam Army infantry and a sister- in-law much too friendly. We all stayed within four to six buildings apart on this road that didn't even have a street sign, so I never got to know its name, but I knew how to get to it from all four directions. Bro. Gator Man made sure I learned that also.

So, with my gun, new apartment room, direction from all directions, I was all over town ready (sure I was) rules in over town after dark were that there were no rules) The streets cleared! Only fools out some nights were Bro. Gator Man and me, the cyclo drivers and hoods. Thank God for Smith & Wesson and Mr. Colt, or we wouldn't have made it back to the good ole USA, and thanks to Bro. Gator Man for double clipping information (really). But we braved the storms and even got to walk about as one of the people after a while. I got to know a lot of good people, starting with the shop keepers and market vendors and cycle men; plus, Ms. Lon's brother was a part time cowboy when not playing infantryman. He would stick a white GI up as fast as he would see him.

Now all of my time was not devoted to over town, no way because Hue' didn't like being left out of the picture. She had designs on me now. You know people would talk, "Walker has butterflied" (found another girlfriend) and she would have to take out a contract on me with the Cowboys (but I was smart!) She didn't have a picture of me, to get copies made off to pass around (I stayed clear of the cameras) oh yea! So, I split my time between Tra-Mai Kei and over town and Plantation Road with Bro. Rochester and Bro. Gator Man and the good times. You know, I don't remember doing at lot of sleeping during the entire three years tour over there but I did nod a lot.

Now, not knowing how Hue' really felt about me way up over town. I found out when she told me about a room for rent just off of 115 & Tru Minn Kie way and it was cheap and across from a market and a bakery and near the main drag. The owner of the house was seemingly middle class. The house had a garden in the front with a fountain, a huge double door and an. outdoor kitchen just off the courtyard with a guard tower overlook built into the front face of the building. This place was nice. The place was renting for 2,000 pee or $25 a month. This amount also gave me the run of the entire house and cooking rights, plus sleepovers for guest girls. Well, it didn't take too much convincing, I took the room. Plus, it was just a block or so away from Hue's house. So, the plan was to wait for Bro. Gator Man to come pass in the morning to pick me up in a cyclo and we would ride to Newport, then off to Long Bien Post, about a half an hour ride, work for 8-10 hours, check in at the Barracks, then catch the bus back to Newport, cyclo to Saigon City and downtown, Saigon or Long Bien Post. I could sleep anywhere, it's all Viet Nam! After a few days and nights of this routine, it turned into old hat. Weeks turned into months.

     Now, staying on this end of town had its benefits. MPs didn't come around much, this was the people's area and they were left alone to govern and police their own area. If you weren't considered a soul brother in good standing, you had better not get caught in the 267, 268 or 269 area. You could get killed! Or beat almost to death. One had to have ties with the neighborhood and its people, and then you still had to watch your back because you were still the enemy, a GI! Every night some fools would either stumble, or be lured into the off limit areas and get killed or beat badly by Cowboys and that would be considered their bad luck! Dummies, mostly white boys or new guys to Nam. The infantry guys back from the field were feared by all of the people because they were wild! They were afraid of nothing and most of the time were looking for a fight or something to fuck up.

     The area was known as Buddha's Shrine or Soul Alley which meant ruled by Blacks! The entire area even though Vietnamese people, Cambodians, Chinese, Thai live and owned houses, stores, markets and everything else was ruled by black GIs. Some were deserters, some that were AWOL and just soldiers and other branches of servicemen. Buddha's Shrine belonged to (Mein Dan) black Men! Whites entered at their own risk! The MPs didn't mess around in here! This place had a thousand alleys, hiding places and each was a trip. Areas had different Dapts, rules and jammed with girls! Some whores, pickpockets, tricksters of all kinds, smoking dens, massage houses, black market vendors, money changers, short time and long time rooms for rent for sex. It even had soul kitchens for food ran by the NCOs from the surrounding Posts that were cooks. Yea, 267 was the gateway to black Viet Nam overseas, and now I had really found out where this town came together.

Now being in a better position to court Hue', I got better settled in. I often walked the area. Now walking about and being able to understand the lingo helped a lot. I would hear the people talking about me, come to find out they had a make on me. I mean a complete make on me! What time my light came on in the morning, when Bro.Gator Man came to pick me up. When I came and when I left out, who I talked to, even when Hue' and her accompanying mob came pass and that Hue' was my min-non (sweetheart), and I was love sick for her without knowing it. Then, I was safe out there most of the time because of my relationship with Ms. Hue' It made me be halfway accepted by the people, but I had something else going on. Without knowing the people were looking at how I treated the street kids, homeless children, loving all over the neighborhood.

I would stop pass the mess hall everyday during lunch and dinner time and get fruit and sweet stuff, stash it at the Barracks and bring it down to Saigon each night and give it to the hungry kids, and I would have some of them run errands for me from time to time and I paid good 100 pee (a lot of money) to them. That 100 pee could feed 8-10 kids, soup, bread and sweet cones (snow cones). I liked the kids. They were real victims of the war, just kids. When I came out in the morning to meet Bro. Gator Man, we would see kids, sleeping in piles of trash in doorways, sleeping in alleys and stuff. Boys and little girls, sad, real sad. It got so Bro. Gator Man also started to get rations to give to the kids, also. We even started to collecting uniforms of the guys leaving Nam going home to give to the kids and man they could work with the material. The shirts could be made into skirts and little dresses for the girls and the boys cut the pants down to fit them. I took a real liking to four kids and made them my stepchildren as Bro. Gator Man called them. They were sharp. Bro. Gator Man and me gave them everything. We fed them until they were almost fat! We got them clothes from downtown Saigon. Their pajamas were silk, they had four and five pairs of flip flops of different colors, barrettes, their own hairbrushes and combs, hair stuff. The two boys had white and black pajamas, leather sandals and yo-yos (Duncan), plus they kept 50 pee in their pockets and most of all (they got to ride all over Saigon in the cyclos with us whenever we went and all of the people saw that. The only shortcoming to that was they told Ms. Hue' everything I did and where we went (little spies) was what they were! But I loved them. Things were going alright for me.

    I had made plans to jump Hue's bones. shit , it had been long enough of this courting stuff. Her bones were going to be jumped! But how to get rid of her mob, those little hussies who went wherever she went? Now, I owed one of the three a debt she had caught me coming out of this girl's house I had jumped one evening and nothing had ever been said about it, but she and I knew what had come off, so that was our secret but every now and then she gave me this look when my eyes would wander as fine girls went pass. But we were cool. The real little one, well a couple of snow cones and 5 pee would do her, but that middle one, she was smart and watched everything and I knew she would be a rock! G4 wouldn't move her. I would have to use the Smith and Wesson or Brother Colt on her. I often wished she would get kidnapped or something at times. I had to find her weakness and play it to death, for this big move I was planning. Bro. Rochester, Bro. Gator Man and myself brainstormed on how I was going to jump Ms. Hue'. Surprisingly, Bro. Rochester even joined in hitting a "Jay" with us. Sitting up there stoned, we had a good time, talking on how to jump her and slip the kids. So, we decided on the movies or the zoo, each of these two gave me a way to slip away with Hue' while Bro. Rochester and Bro. Gator Man and their girlfriends kept the kids off my back (yea) this could work, but we had to put their girlfriends down with the plan. The guys were sure they would get their girlfriends to go along but to leave the part out about me jumping Hue's bones. Just tell them we wanted some time totally alone together. Well, it took days to get any results, but it was a go. I asked Ms. Hue' about the outing. Yes, was her response back in two days, it was on.

Chapter 10
Trip to the Zoo

Now, I had never been to the zoo, but I had gone to the movies in Nam and neither was I planning on being in any longer than a minute. I wanted to take Hue' off. Plus, Bro. Rochester and Bro. Gator Man wanted to have me shut up about jumping that woman! Then I thought when I ducked the kids where was I going to take her, not to my place. The entire area would know in ten minutes, not to Bro. Gator Man's, sure not to Bro. Rochester's barracks, where? Not to downtown Saigon, oh, I know Cho-Lon. Yea! Cho-Lon, the Chinese section. No one knows either of us there. Get a short room, jump and then back to our area, no harm done. But first she had to consent to all of this, but I could make it come off. Well, the day was at hand, all parties were in place, there were eight cyclos, me and Hue', Bro. Rochester and his girl, Bro. Gator Man and Ms. Lin, my stepchildren and her spies, on to the zoo. Man, there was about a thousand people there. Bro. Gator Man bought the kids all blue balloons with white stripes. We gave them 50 pee each and they disappeared. After being told to meet up back at the big brown bear's cage. They flew off. If I had only knew, I would have come to the zoo long ago. We laughed and shook our heads and they ran off to Lord knows where. In that zoo, all eyes were on Hue' and me for a minute, then I started walking and she followed behind at a short distance. Remember GIs and Vietnamese women were not to be together in public unless the GI had papers on her! We caught separate cyclos and off to Cho-Lon. Along the way Hue's cyclo disappeared behind me and I thought she had changed her mind, but the driver looked back at me and smiled and speeded up and at a cross section of a road Hue's cyclo pulled just ahead of mine.

So at the gateway of Cho-Lon, I could see all of the buildings. I said motel, my driver shook his head and speeded up again, passed Hue's cyclo and it followed us to the grand looking place. It looked like a temple or something until I saw sailors, GIs, Air Force men of all ranks all about. Oh yea, this is the place (I thought). No sweat! We pulled up, two attendants aided us in getting out of the cyclos. Hue' still behind me followed me up the grandstand case into this place that was beautiful. Pictures all over the walls, the ceiling, the marble floor, four large rooms laid out before us. This long hallway that led to who knows where.

This place was laid out. Wow! I went to the desk, before I could say a thing the desk clerk asked for my travel card. Travel card? "Yes, your card please". As not to appear dumb, I pulled my wallet, got the card, gave it to him. He looked at it, looked at me, then said sign here please. Unsure, I signed the book, he reached and gave me a room key. Wow, I was blown away. He pointed toward the long hallway I had saw and said "The lift is at the right near the white column, Sir." So, I started to walk slowly that way. Hue' followed as I walked the hall. I noticed signs with rules on them. Come to find out this building was ran by the U.S. Navy. It was a Naval brothel and massage hall ran by the Armed Forces here. The girls worked legal, got checked by doctors for any diseases, gave massages, worked as call girls, strippers or entertainers, as they called themselves and paid fees to the Vietnamese government for the honor. Boy, the Navy had it going on!

Officers all over the place from all forces and civilians everywhere and to think of some of the dives I had been tricking at. I had to hip Bro. Rochester and Bro. Gator Man to this spot. But, first to jump Ms. Hue'. Thinking all things had come together, I began to check the huge room out. There was a huge window dead in the middle of the room as we came in, iron birdcage bars, a large dresser to the left, a bureau to the right, the oversize bed with a canopy with a foot stool at the bottom sitting on a pretty rug.

Two large fans turned slowly above, an extra big wardrobe, double door up against the door next to the toilet room with shower (nice). Hue' looked about, opened the double door wardrobe, there were gowns upon gowns, all colors of the rainbow. She touched and moved them about, then looked back at me. I sat on the side of the bed quiet and just looked. She took out a light green sheer gown and went to the shower room. Jimmy quick, I undressed to my shorts. The door opened, Hue' came slowly walking out of the doorway. Man, the sun coming in the room set that gown off! She looked, she looked great! She perched herself on the bed near the huge pillows. I didn't want to bum-rush her, but I really did want to. We talked a little.

Now what that part of the conversation was only the walls knew, cause I don't remember but as things got hot, Hue' said to me, Walker, I am a cherry girl. Cherry girl! was all I heard. My God! Of all of the women, young girls in Nam, I end up with a Cherry girl. A virgin! Now, the rules were never be caught alone in Nam, never venture in the off limit areas unless except by the people. Keep your mine together no matter how high you got and the big one, no messing with a Cherry Girl! These girls were either children or young women saving themselves for marriage. Yes, marriage. One man forever mostly their own man, their own kind. The old way of life and living over there. Man, I didn't know what to do or say. I just sat there, she sat there in that beautiful gown, naked as sin with her head hung down. Then whispered "Walker you no longer want Hue'? You no longer love Ms. Hue' anymore Walker?" She kept on calling me as if I had moved or walked away or something. I was thinking on what to do. I reached down picking my uniform up from the floor slowly getting re-dressed. I told her to put her clothes back on. She slowly got up and returned to the shower room. I could hear her crying from within standing on the little window tier landing I looked out over the landscape thinking, I had a girl here that was going to give up all she believed in, even to be shunned by her family, even being considered no better than a bar girl or a street girl if she lost her cherry to a GI, black or white and no decent Vietnamese man would want her or pay a dowry for her hand in marriage, plus to loose her cherry to me, I would own her, and if she strayed I had the right to kill her for *butterflying* according to Nam's law. This was a serious situation at hand. Now, Hue' and I were both sitting aside one another. She took my hand rubbed it gently and spoke Vietnamese. "I love you Walker. I love you Walker, more than life itself, sweetheart," which really messed me up. I don't know how much time passed just sitting there. But I decided it was time to go.

We walked back down that long hall to the desk clerk, gave up the key, my mind still in a cloud about where, and what to do next. It was an extra long ride back to 1110 Tru Minn Kie 267 area. We dismounted our rides and took different ways back to Hue's block only to almost arrive at the same time. As I turned the corner at the top of the block, it seemed everyone was either sitting or standing in their doorways like something had happened. Then I saw Ms. Hue' almost to her front, then her mom, Ms. San appeared in her doorway. Hue' stopped short of the front door, then proceeded slowly. The kids came to meet her, taking her hand and hugging her waist. I walked slowly, listening to hear anything said by her mother or others. Nothing, absolutely not one word was spoken by a soul!

As Hue' cleared her mother's front door, Momma Son, Hue' called, "Walker" almost clear as any American could call, "Walker!" She then motioned for me to come her way. "Come here!" And I did. Upon reaching the doorway, she motioned for me to enter her house. I was shocked, but I knew something was suppose to come off, like we had a date, had ducked the kids. The kids returned without Hue' and here we were, how late from getting back? What shouldn't I expect. Once inside the front room, I was pleasingly surprised there was a living room like mine in the USA. Big sofa and chairs, pictures of all these folks, kids, young people, old people, soldiers, a old time radio box, a prayer table with food and water and incense burning. It was real crazy in here, homelike and smelled good.

Hue' was nowhere in sight. Momma-Son motioned for me to sit down and then she disappeared also. I could hear voices, rise and then settle, rise again, then both of them came into the room. Hue' had changed clothes, had on a Chinese robe, she sat. Momma-Son sat down. Then in perfect English, Momma Son said "Walker, Mein Dan, you no love Ms. Hue'? Mein Dan Walker, you no want Ms. Hue'? You no love sick Ms. Hue' Walker, Mein Dan Walker?" Then I guess filled with emotion, the Vietnamese took over and her mouth was going a mile a minute. I couldn't keep up with what she was saying but she was hurt. I broke up the chatter, saying, "Yes, I love Hue', I do." Now looking at Hue' to quell her mother getting off, the woman hyped up was back and forth, rocking and moaning and stuff. I just sat there. Hue' hadn't moved yet.

Then, this woman came from the inner room, that I did not know, nor had I ever seen her before. She was another worker from one of the offices at the Embassy and her English was better than mine. She spoke slowly and calmly, saying "Walker, I am Ms. Lee, Ms. Hue' is my family and my aunt is very upset you and my cousin are thought to be in love. Do you love my cousin, Ms. Hue' Walker? Do you really love Hue' at night and at day and at all time, Walker? Will you love Ms. Hue' when you leave Viet Nam, Walker? You go home and forget Ms. Hue'

Walker, right? You forget Viet Nam and all Viet Nam people, right Walker? Tell Ms. Hue' Walker, tell Ms. Hue Walker, Mein Dan , tell Ms. Hue Walker. Ms. Hue' always love Walker. Ms. Hue' always love Mein Dan too much Walker." This woman was direct, serious and mostly speaking the truth, but I had not thought that far ahead. I was just living day to day. This stuff was heavy. I sat there, then Hue' spoke, "Walker number one, Ms. Hue' gave herself to Walker". Momma Son's head rose. The woman Ms. Lee looked as to say , What?! Ms. Hue' gave herself to Walker, Ms. Hue' still cherry girl. Ms. Hue' love Walker Mein Dan, number one. My Min-nor Walker. This statement made the room still.

Nothing more was said for minutes. Momma Son rose, left the room quietly. Ms. Lee still quiet. Hue' sat next to me close, then Momma Son came back into the room, said come! Looking at all of us unsteadily, I stood as I got a nod from Hue' and followed her into the inner room. It was a dining area, kitchen with a harp open cooking place. The pots and skillets were on the rack. The low table had dishes all around it and a huge bowl of rice was the centerpiece. Momma-Son motioned to sit, we did. She then emptied the pots and skillets into the big bowls on the table. I was going to bread and food down with the family. Yes, like a family member. I was in! Like it or not, it was understood I was to be tolerated. I was Ms. Hue's choice and most of all I had respected their ways. Their cousin, their daughter was still with her cherry and I was a man of honor and really loved her daughter. Hue' explained this all to me and now she could give herself to me fully come what may. If I left Nam, her, the people, she would always love Mein Dan Walker forever her Min-Nor Walker.

I learned a lot that day, how love was looked at by people that were under a lot of stress and how a little bit of happiness if only for a short time was worth it. And I thought on that every time I saw another couple over there in love, knowing it probably wasn't going to last any longer than the GIs ETS date and then home for him. It wasn't too much longer, Ms. Hue' and I got together. We were a real couple. I even had a scare in between Hue' and I becoming a pair. I had just gotten off the bus from Long Bien Post one evening, ready to catch a cyclo. There was a bunch of cowboys parked and cowboys meant trouble. The cyclo driver was on guard and all of the people had moved over from the group of motorcycle hardheads.

As I sat down in the buggy, one of the cyclo, bike pulled right in front of the buggy I was in. The driver pulled his helmet up and it was Phan-Lung Hue', Ms. Hue's brother. Now, was I to be killed or to get the hell beat out of me or just get all broke up and beat up real good? All of this went through my mind in seconds. Lung called, "Walker, Lai Day (come here), Lai Day Walker." I got up, walked over, only to find that he was offering me a ride. He and these thugs were there to escort me down the roads to Saigon City. It was a trip, the dust flying, motors loud, and there was this black guy on the back of a cowboy's bike for all of the people to see. When we hit the City gates, heads turned and fingers pointed, Mein Dan and the cowboys, unheard of and when we hit middle town, black GIs seeing this threw power chicks like crazy and cried Brother Mein. They drove up to Wong Quang Dien & Tru Minn-Kie and I dismounted, brushed the dusk off and styled down the block like some kind of super star! Until today, I don't know if Hue' told Phen Lung to come to Newport or not.

Now as all this was happening, work was still going on for me and my outfit. We were going through some hard times. The North Vietnamese were on the move, they had attacked firebases in the North and the South and it was getting to be an everyday watch. The Cobra's gunship were deployed on 24 hour tours. Ammo was flying out to the firebases like crazy. Some towns, villas were off limits to all GIs and civilians. It was getting hot and most of all Saigon Sal was on the horn every night, calling shots to watch out and damn if she wouldn't be right on with her warnings. Like Camrone Bay had hit the dust sappers and North Vietnamese regulars had done a job on the Posts and damn near leveled the Ammo depot. Messages had been sent to the USA and the ships were on their way. Some converted Germany and Cambodia. My favorite ship was the Falcon Blazer and Vulcan Freighter. I had a lot of communication with them, they brought in the big stuff, 105 mm and 255 mm . The firebases and small arms to protect the bloods on the ground. At times, I felt that I should have been out in the field with the brothers getting a true hit of what Nam was all about (not knowing it was coming). The office was a beehive of activity. Some nights I had to remain on Post and rise early to work my desk. Phone calls to Saigon had to be cleared so contact with Hue' was at a minimum like there was a war going on. Plus, these times gave me Post time with the bloods finding out what was going on Post wide. It was always good to know about the Post things getting worse, race related wise.

There was a clannish climate developing. Small wars from within were going on. Even among the line troops. Once in from the field, whites went their way, Blacks and Chicanos, Hispanics, grouped together and smoking dope had changed to shooting dope. GIs were getting stuck up during the daytime. The MPs and COs were conducting raids on Barracks looking for drugs, even reefer was considered taboo. Pills had hit the Post, immunocal and minnocal or (slammers) like Valium but 4 times stronger had been the drug of choice for many a GI now and they were put into a real stupor, drunk as a skunk! Plus shooting 95% Heroin, whew... too much to think about! And someone had thought how to make the barrels it come in look filled only to find out air pockets of the plastic gave the impression of being full. One had to watch what he bought and some barrels were filled with soap powder, not Heroin. Yes, being a closed Post made dope a commodity to have money to have by selling the stuff and the Post was really getting corrupted.

Some black GI's had got together and robbed the main Post Office on the hill across from USAV headquarters desk log. The rumor was they were deserters from down in Saigon City. This made them some serious guys, so the 716 MP group plus the 504th MP group were both involved in looking for them. This meant also all of the buses leaving the Post along with all other vehicles were to be checked before leaving Long Bien Post. This surely cramped me coming and going so I had to stay on Post. Now Bro. Rochester was still working in Saigon, Clark and I basically were still working at Long Bien Post, working there but sleeping and funning downtown.

At times, I wondered how we were pulling it off and for such a long period of time. Things loosened up and we went back to our routine. Work, riding the bus to Newport, then get a cyclo down to the City, but with a big change. We met a young Sergeant who was doing some big time hustling. He worked the docks at Newport and was selling the drink of the country, Cognac Hennessey. Hennessey was used to make the famous Saigon tea only $5.00 a fifth but sold on the black market for $55 = $4,100 on some days according to demand and supply and he commanded a control unit of supplies. Tons and tons sent over from the USA. Food, cigarettes, liquor, uniforms, the entire nine yards and all types of invoices came through his hands and here we were.

Upon meeting him and getting tight with the brother was a blessing because he knew the docks and we knew Saigon City. Now to make things even better, munitions, bullets, ammo of all types had to be trucked out of Newport and guess who knew how and where to get the placards to fit the jeeps and three quarter trucks he had at his disposal. By the way the Sarge was named Chambers, Sergeant Chambers of Charlotte, NC, twenty year old son of a Baptist preacher and straight as an arrow. He didn't smoke, nor drink yet. But, that would change, oh boy did that change. Well, we were into smuggling liquor by the three quarter ton in our Army truck right down the street from Ms. Hue's house. There lived Ms. Tee-Hy on the neighbor black market fences, she was big time around there, a big house, large garden, three motorcycles, a big bird cage with expensive birds in it of all colors and a caged little spider like monkey. But most of all her husband was a Colonel in the Vietnamese Army in Intelligence and everybody respected or should I say was afraid of him. One word from him and you could go to jail forever but he couldn't touch us GI's, only his people.

We belonged to the good ole US of A GIs, you know, hands off! He and Tee-Hy were crooks from a bar of soap to a tank, they would buy if given the chance. If we could get it, they would buy it or arrange to get whatever bought. Well, every case of Cognac we got, we sold it to them, 24 bottles per case $2,400 in a clip, split between the some times four of us, Bro. Chambers, Bro. Gator Man, Bro. Rochester and me. But sometimes only one of the three of us or two of us. It varied, but times were good and at times it would be anything Bro. Chambers got his hands on to sell, not always liquor. The money was rolling in which made it easier for me to spend and send more money home. I was sending money orders home like crazy. My sister Delnora was starting college and kids were entering junior and senior high school and I was funding the way for them, plus helping Mama with taking care of them. Plus, Mama wanted to move so money was needed. Also, I was going to get Ms. Hue' and I a place of our own. By now I had made up my mind that I was never going to come back to the USA, not ever. I liked Viet Nam. I liked it over in Asia, war or not! I was thinking and looking around right down the street, just five doors way from where I was staying. There was a building that had burnt down. I found out the lot was for sale. I talked to Hue' about it. She checked it out and found out the lot was up for sale. She also told me we could get it and build a house on the lot for us and make babies. The cost was cheap being the money ratio was 8 to 1 meaning 8 of their dollars for every 1 of USA dollars but it had to be USA $100 bills with the red crescent reef on the bill.

 Well, I started to have $100 bills sent over from home to me just for the purpose of buying this lot plus building a home for us, the entire price would be about $24,000 in their money, a fortune for them so I began working towards that. The money was flowing in and I had one of the GIs in the drafting office on the hill make me blueprints of what I wanted built. I started to send for stuff from the Sears and Wards catalogs. I had all of the supply unit Sergeants I knew stealing all kinds of stuff. I had boxes all over the front lawn of where I stayed and in the back of Hue's mother's house. I even had a hot water heater and refrigerator and freezer, a propane stove with six burners, air conditioners, color televisions, lava lamps, ming vases, name it, I had it already. The workmen started and worked like ants. The three story frame went up like a dream, it had a sunken cellar with plumbing straight down to the sewage line. I had the traditional rain trap tank on the roof for stored water, but I had Western toilets, not the hole in the floor Asian type to bend over stooping to take a crap and I even had a generator for electric gasoline ran plus a hook up line to the City electric poles. My roof top porch had two parts to it, one side opened, the other side closed to keep the Monsoon out, plus it was to be screened in. But, first I had to get papers on Ms. Hue' because a GI couldn't even walk in public with her without papers. But that meant that I would have to confess to all of the people that I loved her and had intentions of marrying her and supposedly would take her to the USA. Well, no sweat! I went and got the papers, $500,000 Piasters to $500 American, later she was mine. I could hold hands with her in public, ride together in a cyclo for all Vietnam to see. She was mine, I was her man to tell all of the people. We were one. But I still wasn't married to her yet, but promised, so no messing around or die for sure!

So with all of this going on, we had forgot about the Major, Hue's boss. Now, as I said he lived in the Officer's quarters, the big apartment building right across the street from where I was having the house built. He was aware and watching all of this and still very much in love with my pretty and smart bride to be. He was scheming on how to put a monkey wrench into all of our plans. The dirty dog began once again to hound my woman, even questioned her about her intentions and warned her I would leave Nam without her, only hurt her, play with her heart. He even told her he loved her and wanted to marry her himself and had more to offer than me. This chump was serious and as fate would have it, I lucked up and got another temporary tour of duty at MACV Headquarters and bullet at

Plantation Road. Oh boy, to really mess up his plans to separate the two of us apart. That must have blown his mind when he saw me walking down the hall with orders of assignment to the duty log. He probably wanted to croak me on the spot. Now, I was back in Saigon on assignment with Bro. Rochester. Bro. Gator Man's tour was almost over, but he decided to extend his tour for a year and did so. He even demanded a reassignment to the Medical Center in Saigon and got it. Man, all three of us were together plus Bro. Chambers, our new partner in crime had now joined us to run the streets and alleys of Saigon together. We were a force to reckon with.

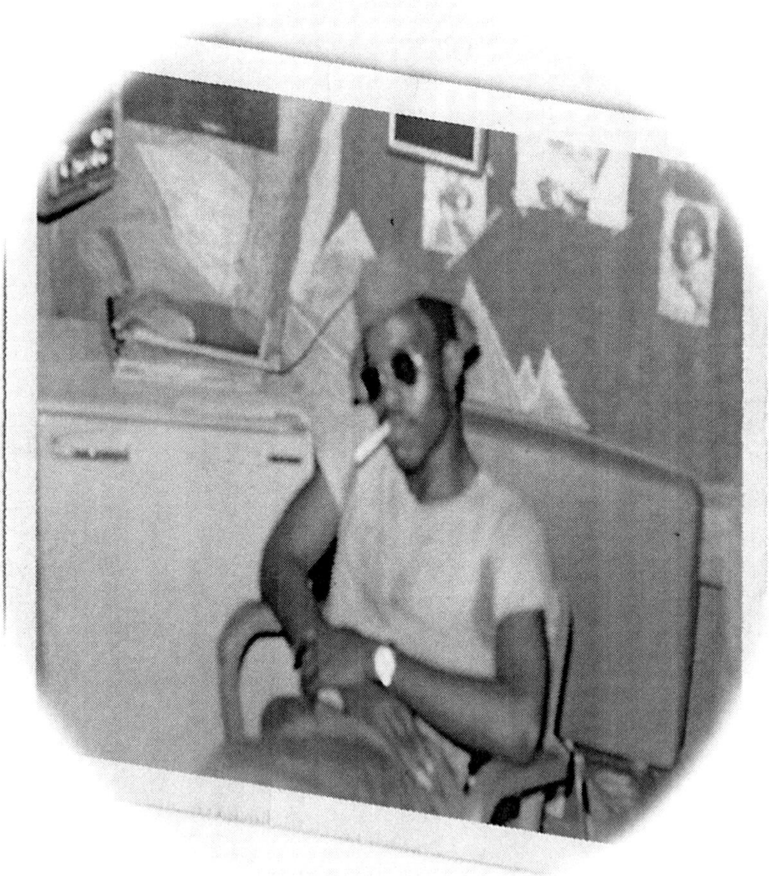

Chapter 11
My New Home

     Time seemed to slow down for a while. The house, now finished, everything now in place, I moved in and to boot I was going to get married, really married. Now, I had already started practicing to be a Buddhist and had started to get the paper work started for Hue' with the Army for marriage and a Visa, but I didn't know she had told most of her friends, relatives and work mates about our plans and I didn't know she was pregnant either, did I say knocked up! Yes, I did, but then to my surprise out of nowhere, orders to go to Phu-Bia up North. Where, why Phu-Bia, why? To inventory how many firebases and small ammo supply point up North? That many! Man shit! How many?! And stay how long? Why me? Well, I found out shortly that damn guy, the dirty dog, he had pulled strings and got his way! The Major had used his connections and favors as I was told just to get at me and took aim and fired and got his kill, me! I was going on a tour all the way up North. He even laughed in my face as we passed in the hallway and even saluted me one time. But I fought back

     Within 3 days, I road down 1110 Tru Minn Kie on a white pony with Ms. Hue' on a brown pony with a too-too band with it seemed like the entire city of the people dancing and setting off firecrackers and yelling. I was married to Ms. Phen Thi Hue'. Now, Mrs. GI Nathaniel Obie Walker, Jr, SP5, US Army. Not only married but daddy to be, but not many knew of the baby coming at the time, not even Hue's mom. I told Bro. Rochester, Bro. Gator Man, Bro. Chambers, then her mother, brother, my Captain Thomas and a few hundred close friends about me going to be a father but I was cool with it. I called home to tell my mother and sisters and brothers and some family members and I was happy.

I made arrangements at Tan Son Nhut Air Force base for a pass to get on Post for Hue' and a pass to use the Veterans' Hospital for she was now my spouse and could get treated like a GI and I wanted everything to be in place while I was gone to insure Hue's and the baby's health, so I did. Then off to Phu Bia and the war effort again. I got up North after a stop off in Da Nang, then up to Phu Bia, stayed in the processing station for a week. Then on to the Company Ane 426 S&S Bn Desk Log Ammo HQ & HQ Company A. A big outfit, with a very large area to cover with many a firebase to inventory. First off the First Sergeant asked me what I had done wrong to get sent up there from Saigon and said "Son, you will never get to go back down South son." I almost dropped to my knees. The Company area was a mess, old, dirty, crowded, smelly, and war-torn.

The GIs looked just as bad, these guys looked like a bunch of rejects. The barracks were shabby, the shower was a shame, it housed a shitty sprinkler system and was gasoline mercer can heated. The outhouses were a joke and the Post for the 101st GI's had no women at all allowed as a standing order! No women allowed, none. This place had incoming rounds, three times a day and a 24 hour guard mount and stayed on alert. Well, welcome back into the war. I thought welcome. The Major had really fixed my goat. I was up and working six hours upon getting there on the front line setting and checking charges, setting claymore mines and inventorying records. They had a job for me to do and I was doing it ASAP and bad as it was I had to work with NG's straight out of Redstone Arsenal, fresh off the plane, that I didn't know nor trust one bit. But this was the job.

I was housed with all of these white boys, the only Brother in the hooch (barracks) and white boy music. Man, I was ready to go AWOL already! Tired, I thought I was going to get some sleep when I heard a chopper landing right outside the door. The hooch was right at the base of a heliport, all night they came. Me, the only person awake in the joint, still unpacked wondering how I got here and hungry. The Mess Hall damn near a quarter mile across the Post, an entire Battalion to feed, guys running to get their thirty minutes to eat and man, I had to make formation up here, formation I had never seen anything like this, there was this giant hill. In the middle of the Post, all faced it for one of three formations, so many men. I had to learn this Post, but I could see another part of the Post that was different, it was support group areas way different from the restrictive area of the 101st area. They had more relax type of living arrangements and most interestingly they had women, hooch girls, wash women, plenty of them all about.

These guys all had their own women working for them, more than we had on Long Bien Post. They even during the evening pimped the women off to the infantrymen of 101st and the girls were in demand at all times. I was working like a dog! Assigned to a Philly Pad (helicopter group and a shithook outfit - Chinook, a large cargo helicopter). I did all I was trained for back in the USA at Redstone Arsenal (ammunition, explosives, missiles, renovation, record, retrograde) school and believe me I wore all of those titles and worked them at a calling, no questions asked. I was a soldier! Up here in the North I was getting to earn my "brownie points" and to really learn what this war was about! But the big difference came when I had to board a chopper to go to a firebase that was not like any I had ever seen. Not a huge mountain, ant hill like thing, but a flat piece of land with steel boxes buried in the ground with the gun on top out in the open, shells piled up to the side bunker and dirt barriers all about with bunker lanes chopped out in an ant form maze that stretched out it seemed for miles and the GIs were ragged as a bowl of Yat Gaw Mein or damn near naked but seemingly alright with how they were living out there, use to it, 101 mm guns all about.

Within the premises, the connick boxes for ammo were well stocked with small arms, ammo, and other dirt burned bunker spaced just as the textbooks we had learned from, perfect and well kept. But this Post was in the wide open spaces just out there! Tree lined and shrubbery way off in the distance, barbed wire, ditches, claymores, trip flares, cans on the wire, all kinds of junk hanging on the wire even a naked doll baby hanging. This was GI owned territory. I just looked about and took all of the sights in. We got the once over by the deaf (artillery men) and after awhile it chilled and us GI's talked to one another. Most of the brothers joked about how loose our shit would be when they would start to go to the hole later that evening (firing) up hill to kill Mr. Charlie, (North Vietnamese) but they didn't know we had seen and heard the smoke before down south (or at least I had) but like all of the other GIs over there we were young, didn't let anything get too serious, so we joked a lot. During the three days there we made a few friends, inventoried, then skied up. Now back two hours to Camp Eagle or the Eagle's Rest HQ & HQ 101st Airborne/Air Mobile Battalion (Camp Eagle Vietnam, South) all missions and reports started and stopped there. We stayed hours filling out reports, then ate chow, showered and crashed out.

      Now was my time to relax, write a letter home, and plot on how to get an assignment to go back down South were I felt I really belonged, which stayed on my mind. At night now I would take long walks, learning the Post and each time I'd go on a walk, it was a trip. Nobody slept, soldiers all over the roads, sitting out, sitting out getting high, little firefly like lights flickered on and off from the "Jays" that were being smoked and the air thick with the smell of Reefer and Heroin, radios playing, tape decks with all types of music you could hear coming at you from all sides. But it all was good. I'd just walked until I'd find myself back at the Company area again and wait for daylight. Monsoon was upcoming, that meant a long stay inside for everyone, no helicopter flying, a lot of lifts to the field would be limited for the Infantry groups and truckers and hopefully a lot less shots for the firebases but a bigger problem for drug addiction for us GIs and more diseases passed around because less women would be allowed on the Post for security purposes. The bases still had to be inspected and that meant work for me and my Attachment

Company, and we did fly. I became the man up North each time I'd hit a L-Z I was loaded with barrels of dope all of that traveling back and forth was paying off in big ways for me. I had a young Warrant Officer flying the C130 airplanes back and forth from Saigon. Being down South produced yes, product in the big barrels, Saigon dope, not this up North stuff, that was surely cut with something by the time it was sold to the common GI. Ours was sold just as we got it off the top, 93.99% pure! And the firebases were rocking. Also back at the Company area, I had a couple of stashes being sold by one brother and one Chicano brother and we were killing.

Now, the guys on our side of the Post didn't have to walk across Post to cop, and get soaked in doing so. All was going well, then I received a letter from Bro. Rochester. The news took me by complete surprise. Bro. Rochester talked of the Major hanging around the house even carrying on conversations with Hue's mother, sending PX goods to Hue's mother's house and trying to get close with my house kids, buying little gifts and treats. The Major was launching a campaign of sorts and Bro. Rochester knew I should have wind of it. Now, Hue' was pregnant, about four months and, showing, had a house, money, and married. What the hell was going on? I made my way to the Communication Center the next day, called down Saigon Headquarters, got in contact with Bro. Rochester, Stewart and three more members of my Unit to get in contact with Ms. Hue' to get ready to receive my call. Hue' was contacted and we talked. Hue' told me her job was on her back, she was pregnant, not only pregnant but pregnant by a GI. Seemingly not liked by those in control and as she thought or was thinking the Major could be of help in helping curve the decision on her getting dismissed or may be could influence thinking towards a transfer to another job station and in the same breath shamed me for thinking anything else could cause my dealing with that dinky darr dee wyi damn her (all curse words believe me! In translation). We laughed after I yelled crocodile him Hue' (kill him, kill him sweetheart). We talked on for about ten minutes or so. It was good to hear her voice, hear about the kid, hear about Saigon news, even though I knew about a lot of Saigon's goings on from the Lt. who flew back and forth, up and down country sometimes three times a week. It sounded better coming from her.

    Now cool with what was going on down at the house, I could rest easy. Only to get stressed out again, two members of our kit got blown to hell! Killed, died inspecting the line just outside of the front gate of the Post off of Highway 1. This had the entire Battalion on alert and we worked from sun up to sundown and then on watch all night long. We were told we would have to go on a round to search a village a few miles down the road called Sally. A small, but dangerous little village. GIs were warned to stay out of the area and trucks were told, ordered not to stop but to speed up while traveling through there. Some dumb ass GI would jump off a truck trying to cop some dope and get croaked and cause an alert for weeks at a time but this time other villages were involved in an attack too close to our main Post so the 101st 501 was yelled out and a kit of us tagged along.

    Not long after seeking, we found just what we were looking for, not really in the Ville but in a shanty town that had about a thousand make shift shacks, huts made out of everything that could be found around the area. As our trucks pulled up and men started off loading, setting up a perimeter, people started running about! Who was who? Where was the shooting coming from?! Who was doing what? Everyone was locked and loaded! Then a GI to the left of us dropped! Everybody was now in the melee. People ducked, stood still with their hands held high, yelling crying. GIs running about, pushing folks, yelling, scared out of their minds. It was like a movie but real. And one could get killed and it was not going to be me! Orders were being sounded out to move up and we did. Shots were still being fired down to the right of our position. As we seemed to group close together, the further we got away from the main body of shanty houses and huts but it was still dense with make shift dwellings and too many civilians running all about. Then a shout, "Over here, over here, Gooks"! "Gooks"! Combatants, and we moved like a well-oiled team down this road to another road to the bottom of a lane and there we met plenty of firing.

Chapter 12
Getting Shot in Combat

Action was hot coming from four buildings, two white stone like buildings and two others made of tin and wood like stuff and three men outside shooting and scampering around in between the buildings. Now, they were on the run and we were like a pack of hungry wolves chasing for the fill! Our men had been hit and pay back was in order. Shots rang over and over and as we got closer and closer moving up the hill to the houses. Then I went blank, blank! I don't remember what went on. Next thing I know I am up against a wall, my leg hurts, me and at least four to five other GIs are looking at one another. The signal is that someone is inside this house and firing had been coming from this house and we were going in, then we charged the door! And started shooting as the door bounced up against its back stop. We fired and fired, me being to the left fired to my left and there were two figures to my left and they were the ones doing the shooting. They had shot my GI buddies, had tried to kill us all! The enemies! Killers and I shot and shot until my clip was empty! I was sailing! Out of breath, sweating like crazy. All of us were keyed up. The room was full of gunpowder, smoke and smelled to high hell of gunfire. As I looked around and about the bullet riddled room, my eyes stopped, the shock of seeing these two shapes semi-curled up like a bundle of rags was one white and one black clothed pair of women, one a young girl. A strange gloom was about, no one said a word, we just stood there. It was hot in there, no light seemed to come into the opened door. The noise outside seemed to bring me back to what was going on. I didn't feel bad, or any remorse, I don't think I felt anything. I just walked past who was standing in my pathway until the breeze of outside hit me in the face. I then felt a stinging in my right leg, a kind of sticky feeling on my ankle. I looked down at my feet and got weak in the knees, I almost fell over. I was bleeding, my green sock was tinged red, my pants were bloused so I pulled them up, both legs, yes, I was shot, a hole going right through to the other side. I yelled, "I'm hit!" The next thing I knew I was covered by GIs all about me. Seemed nobody was in charge, but I had plenty of help patching me up. Still not a word was spoken. I half sat, laid there looking at the guys. We all looked wild, a strange look like what had just happened was unreal or tiresome. Then comes the gunship, a slick, but also a weird thing, a Red Cross hospital truck, yes a truck with the big red cross on the side and back doors, unreal. It was coming from up the road at Phu Bia to cart the dead off, bag them, tag them and ship them home, but still I didn't feel anything, like sorry or sad about them leaving dead. I think the whole incident had changed me at that point or was if when the first shot range out. It had all come together for me, not only was I Explosive Ordinance, I was also a grunt Infantryman and Nam would kill me if I didn't look out.

      I then was sitting on a side seat in the van with the black bags holding bodies, no longer GIs, just bodies, for that was how soldiers were to see these bags and be glad not to be in one of them. I remember thinking all I knew was my leg hurt and I wanted a "Sally Jay" filled with a whole barrel of my "shit". The ride was short lived and quiet. We arrived at the field hospital next to 1/501st Company area and the heliport and the medics hauled us hit guys to the blood tents for care. Somebody hit me up with some morphine and I lit up a "Jay" and coasted off to sleep. During my stay in the field hospital, I met a lot of guys and I recuperated. I limped around, exercised and took rehab and wrote letters and then returned to my Company on light duty, working a desk, no questions, no talk about what had come off. But, I carried plenty of mental scars.

Assignments were going out and I wanted to get out of that office and somehow I felt different about being in Nam, and I now disliked Sir Charles, "Charlie", and I felt that I could and would kill if asked or ordered to do so now without any sweat. I had now gained a new status, I had earned my Combat Infantryman badge had two kills. For, I had justified that the guns found in the house had been fired. Our men had been hit by fire coming from that building, and I was a Purple Heart soldier up North Viet Nam near the DMI, and I would kill the Major if he got in my way or didn't leave my wife alone. I would crocodile him for sure!

Then to add to my new me, I got a message I had calls from Saigon while I was in the hospital that no one hipped me to. I was enraged and the Red Cross had not notified my Mom about the incident. I made a call home first from the USO Club then was granted a ten minute call to Saigon to talk to Hue'. I was told she no longer worked there or for the Embassy or where she was working or where she was. I blew my wig! I called Bro. Rochester, he was shocked to hear me on the phone, he thought I was in the States, that I was sent home (safe). He told me he and Bro. Gator Man were stopping pass the house and the kids had gone hog wild, stealing and hustling and stuff. Some people had moved in and was all but running my house. My house was almost a flop house! I asked about Hue's mother. Bro. Rochester said nothing, but she was no help.

I shot back to the Company into the orderly room, broke into first Sergeant's office and demanded leave to go down to Saigon ASAP. After Blade slowed me down, listened to me and what was going on he said he would try to help. Two days later, Blade gave me travel orders, but I was to check into Long Bien Post and be under supervision of the Desk Log Commander and allow him to conduct actions to be taken to resolve my problem.

Well, as soon as I got off that C130 Airship, I headed for Saigon City to take care of my own shit as I saw fit! When I hit 100 Tru Minn Kie, the block was all eyes on me. I had a green towel draped over and around my neck. I had a screaming eagle patch on my sleeve (no screaming eagle soldiers were stationed down South, they were killers from up North). I had a Colt .45 pistol, slung on my left arm, a Viet Nam's Officer's cap on my head (claiming I was in charge of all about me)! And I was looking for a fight!

When I reached the house, a crowd was behind me! The gate to the garden was closed and locked. I kicked the front door open, walked in, the table was jive set, food was in three bowls, one chair turned over, a pot boiling in the dutch oven. I kicked the table over and started up the steps to the second floor. I could hear voices in Vietnamese, Dee, Dee-Dee, Dee (go, go, go!) up the stairs to the flat of the second floor. No one up front, no one in the back bedroom, the middle room empty also. But the rooms were in a mess. Junk all over the place! Nowhere to go but up and I started to slow walk up those 16 steps. I had made my mind up to kill any strangers I would find, man or woman. Their ass was out, I was going to croak them for fucking up my house, enslaving my kids and playing landlords on my piece of the world, Nam or not! This was mine!

I reached the door next to one of the bedrooms, there were three of them and a restroom. I kicked all three of the doors in, no one in them, on to the roof. Now the roof was three stories high, damn near 60 foot to the ground. No jumping off there, here they were all curled up like squirrels in a tree hole, holding on to one another, weeping and moaning and begging "Please Mein Dan, Mein Dan please." I stood there with my pistol cocked, sweaty, keyed up, ready to blow them away as my mind took me back to that damn house, the woman and the young girl all curled up, and me standing there looking at a carbon copy of that day and once again there was noise behind me, but this time it was 716th MPs yelling for me to "Halt! Sergeant, halt, lower your weapon!" "Sarge lower your weapon Sarge". I looked at those bastards, I looked up at the hotel across the street, the window had folks hanging out of every window. They wanted to see GIs killing GIs I thought. But not today. I lowered my Colt to my side, then eased off on the catch, then engaged the safety lever. The two MPs walked up slowly to me, saying "Damn man, what are you doing, trying to start a war or something." I almost laughed, still looking at all of Viet Nam peering from their windows and porch windows from the hotel across the way, but my main focus was on the porch where I knew the Major stayed for it was him I really wanted to kill.

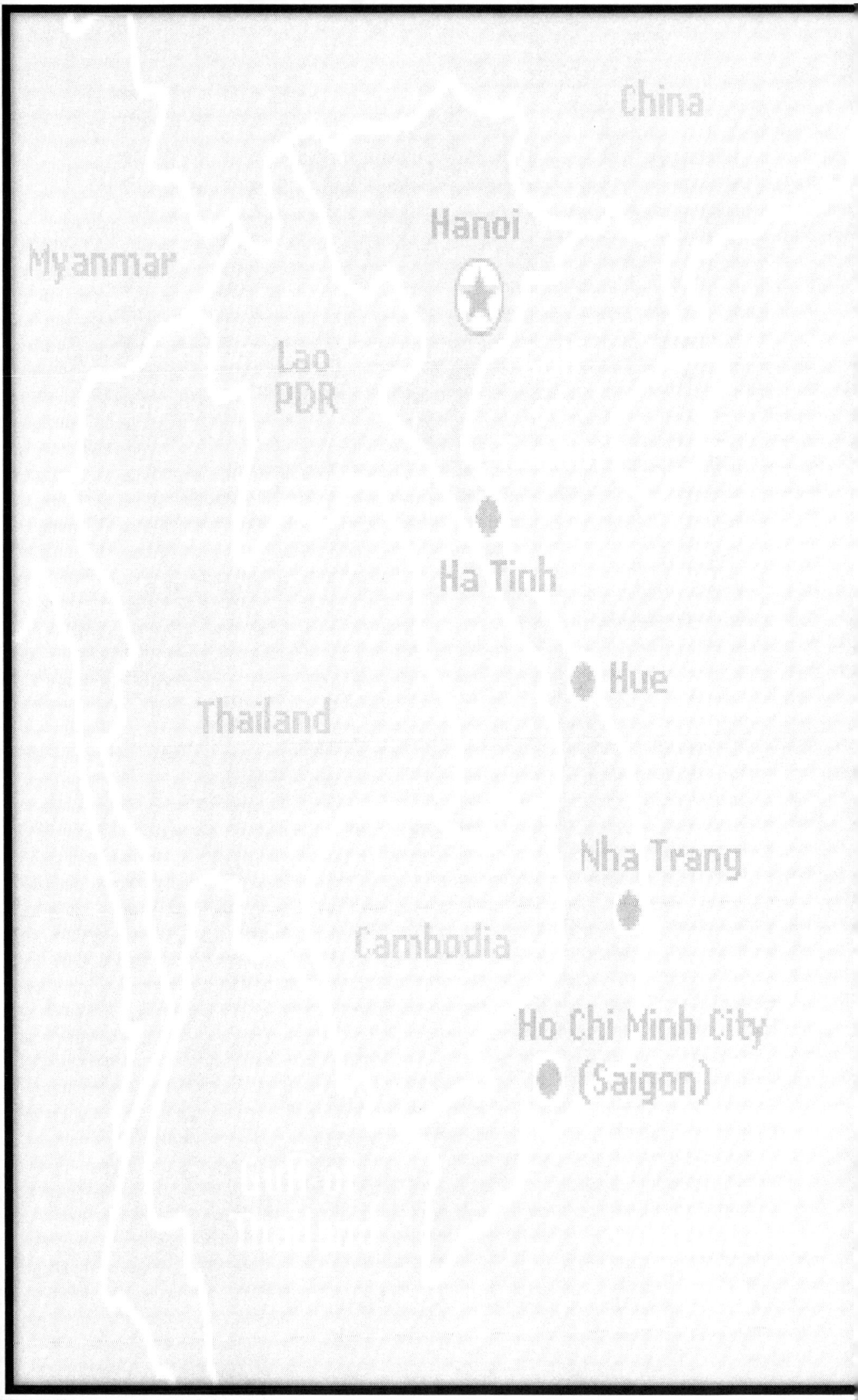
China
Hanoi
Myanmar
Lao
PDR
Ha Tinh
Hue
Thailand
Nha Trang
Cambodia
Ho Chi Minh City
(Saigon)

Chapter 13
Court Martial

Now I was confronted with explaining what the hell had got me off. The MPs gave me plenty of time to tell my story they knew of the black GI that lived here, being me, but had never had a run in with me or any of the other black guys that often came to this house. They knew a lot about this house and what was happening here on this street, but they had a job to do, so they locked me up, telling me that I had no right to pull a weapon on the civilians, threatening their lives even though they had entered my house, took it over without my permission.

I had traveling orders that stated I was to have a non-commissioned officer escort me in my effort to resolve my problem while in Saigon, of which I had no defense I had disobeyed all the stated orders of my headquarters. So, once again I find myself in the back of a MPs jeep, handcuffed. We drove to downtown Saigon Police Headquarters for 716th MP Group. I started to process in, a clerk took my statement of facts, then into a huge outdoor bullpen wire screened with four guard towers manned with 60 caliber machine guns. This bullpen was full with GI men that were charged with AWOL, deserters, killers, thieves, rapists, drunks, black marketers. This was just like the make up of a jail in the world, but these boys could get worse judgments against them because we were in a war zone and guilty until proven innocent, the way the Army see it wrong! I found somewhere to sit and waited to be called to go before the court martial or whatever. Plenty of guys before me got called, but nobody came back to the yard.

Finally, they called me. Three captains sat at a long table. They looked me over as if I was trash or something. One of the young white Officers started,

"What's your name soldier?" I responded with my name, rank, service number and Post Station. "What are you doing in Saigon Soldier?" I responded with my story told, I ended up stating, "My Command was aware of me being in Saigon city to clear my affairs as my orders stated, Sir." The second Officer spoke, "Without an escort Soldier?" "No sir." Was my response. "Why not Soldier?" "I wasn't thinking about an escort sir." The third Officer jumped in, "Soldier, did you resolve your business here in Saigon?" This Officer said my rank. This man was judging me as a soldier and my conduct in the field. I was trained on merits and deeds. This hit me way deep down inside. This gave me a sense of being! I started to thinking who I was, what I had been going through, where I was, what mission I was on! Why I was back down south! Hue', the baby, the house I had built, this fucked up war, the whole fucked up affair. I felt myself righteous! Right on point and I had to get loud, but respectful.

Every word was right on time. The three judges just sat silent, listening to every word. I was sweating and moving all about, getting more worked up second by second. I was real! My mission was uncompleted and I was wronged by the U.S. Army, the way I saw it and only I could make things right. Then abruptly I stopped talking. I was told to exit the hearing room back to the bullpen. The men left in the yard were amazed to see anyone come back to the yard. They asked me what had come off. I stated, "Nothing." I just told the truth about my situation, they seemed to be in awe. It seemed hours passed. I was called back before the panel.

The second Officer spoke, "Sergeant E-5 Walker, you are remanded to the Saigon Region Viet Nam under guidance of MACV Headquarters and Headquarter Battalion until you resolve your affairs, noting you will remove the South Vietnamese Officer's cap headdress, ROC uniform, trousers, 101st Airborne boots and 101st

Airborne jungle shirt with double eagles with the name Wade affixed name tag and wear your own rank and regulation jungle fatigues and you are ordered to report back to this Court upon completion of this event. You are so by ordered!" Man, I could have killed every Mr. Charlie in all of Viet Nam if they had asked me to do so. They had ruled on my behalf. I was beaming with joy as I hollered for a cyclo to get out of dodge, to get to get to the Quartermaster laundry to get a straight USA uniform up at Tan Son Nhut Camp Swamee Army Post.

Once suited up and some chow with my new orders in hand I strutted out the front gate worry free to carry on. I jumped in the first cyclo I saw and back to Tru Minn Kie 110. I had to show the people I was back. I had to take command of my house, my world again. I had to show how strong Mein Dan was to the people, to rise again. Mein Dan strong, but I had to get another gun or two to make me feel complete and I did get some new iron (gun). Now, my research took two days to get a complete picture of what had transpired in my absence and plenty of people were ready to tell me their version. I have now rounded my kids up, back together. They came in cleaning and making the house almost back to its standard. I knew now for sure where my girl and my child was, Da Lat? Da Lat, a province up country! Da Lat on the coast, south of Da Nang, miles and miles away from Saigon City, down here in the south. I had to find a way to get up there.

Now, I knew I was about to disobey orders once again. I began to plot on how to get out of Saigon City, get up to Da Lat, get Hue' and my child, then get them back safe to Saigon without getting a court martial for disobeying my orders again and going to jail! I began to think how, how do I pull this off. So, I thought GIs, yea GIs all over the place, all over. That's how. My brother men! So, I started to talking to brother man upon brother man, everywhere I knew, smoking dens, lunch tables, bars, hooch after hooch, everywhere. Then the feedback began to click. I had bloods talking at me from all over, especially in Buddah's Shrine, Soul Alley. The barbershop was a buzz. I sat down only to hear GIs talking about my plight. These GIs didn't even know they were talking about me and when I spoke up, "I'm the GI you are talking about." Man, I was surprised to the greeting. Man, the small shop was full of young men, all talking to me at once. Bro. this and Bro. that and Bro. did you know this, and man I know this Bro. who works here and he can get you this and that and you can do this. I felt like I had every GI in the country on my side so I got with Bro Blade, Bro. Gator Man, Bro. Rochester and Carl, our Air Force buddy (Carl is a white boy, a friend of Stewart's), who worked at the airport on Tan Son Nhut Airbase to set up my master plan. We met up at my place, the plan was to get boarding passes to first get from Saigon to Da Nang, them from Da Nang to Da Lat up the coast, but we needed transportation from Da Nang to Da Lat, then transportation from Da Lat back to Da Nang, then from Da Nang back to Saigon and that was just for me, not Hue'. She would have to travel ARVN air transportation all of the way. She was not military. I needed travel orders all the way through up and back. Plus to date, none of us knew even were Da Lat really was. But first things first. I had a MP Sergeant Latino type, Sergeant Hernandez from Jersey, cool, hardcore, loved up some smoking dope. The entire U.S. Army knew he liked junk, but the man did his job. He was a true cop. I met him in an opium den off of 123 in the heart of 267 off limits area a year and some days ago. We got to be tight and both us had women whom were Cambodians. Well, he was needed and was requested to help and he did (mad man) as I nicknamed him. He played a very big part from this point on, he got us boarding passes, contacts to get travel orders, even contact people all along our route. I mean like companies to sleep over, clerks that were on the ready to walk us about, show us where the areas came together, transportation, food, sleeping quarters and we did all of this protected by the law, the MP groups.

Now, with all of this help, with all of the aid the brothers were going to get me, as we all knew the end result we would be paying the piper, probably a court martial, lost of all of my stripes, jail even. But it would be worth it. The plan was tight, all that was to do was to do it!

A few days later, after a night where myself and eight others came together at my crib, smoked, talked and fine tuned our plan, all was at the ready set for sun rise and off. The wait for the call to Da Nang seemed to take forever, but it came. I started to board, when I saw more than two faces that were familiar, Bro. Rochester and Bro. Gator Man, then Chewy and Bro. Brown. Bro. Rochester and Bro. Gator Man had duffle bags. They tried their best to get seated as close as they could to where I was seated so we talked aloud from where we sat, and I lie not but by the time we got to Da Nang Airport, we had the entire C-130 airship ready to help or do whatever they could to help us find that woman and her child and get them shipped back to Saigon. I was all messed up with the assistance that was offered me.

Upon landing, straight to the back of a one ton truck and we rode for an hour or two. We stopped at a company area short of billet directed to follow a young GI to a large bay, an Infantry Company, so we were on the edge of a big Support Battalion. We slept there that night, up about mid a.m. and on our way with a transportation convoy carrying supplies, only to another group carrying ammo, onwards and onwards we broke out the Air Fore cee rations, slept among the pilets and bumped on down the road. It seemed forever, then the air changed. The breeze was more moist, hearty. One could smell the salt, the funky fishy smell, we were near water. Peeping from under the tarp of the 2 ½ ton truck, it was obvious we were traveling along the coast of somewhere. The sunrise was half dark blue and black with yellow highlights peering up with a white top trying to make its way to the ceiling of the sky, to reveal everything under, once it had broken through. Now, there was not much to see to the right of us but, plenty to the front. The city laid before us, not of the people of Nam, but one of the U.S. Navy, trucks, jeeps, trailers, helicopters, philly pads, barracks, all over the place, building after building. The patchwork of areas, was awesome to behold with a back drop of a huge mountain range behind all of the manmade real estate.

We pulled down to a gated guarded shack, then entered the compound and drove onwards for a mile or so, stopped, jumped out to some of the nicest barracks I had ever seen. Gray painted, clean, laid out areas. Those sailors (Navy guys) had it good, and better than the Air Force guys. No sooner had we touched down, this Ceebee came out of nowhere to greet us, like we were old friends, called out "Walker, right?" "Reynolds, Bro. Gator Man, right?" Reluctantly, we responded yes.

He guided us to a barrack where we were met by a bunch of men, more than ready to help us. We chowed down in their mess hall, ate from four courses, chose what you want in line, cooked on sight as you wanted it cooked. Steaks, ribs, chicken, pork chops, lamb. All kinds of stuff, and not one kind of drink, but coke, milk, all kinds of sodas. Man, these guys ate good and the living quarters were like home, but better. Steel bunks with fat mattresses, blankets of soft wool, fitted sheets, fat pillows, air condition billets and hot water showers. Well, this was nice but didn't last for long.

The next morning we were gone, bumping along once again in the back of a truck to some town. The smell was much like Saigon, gasoline, dust, noisy, smokey people all about, crowded as hell. Sailors in their white , soldiers in dress khakis, officers all about and (MP) military police, the office workers (Vietnamese) were men and women all dressed mostly American style dress. The truck stopped. One of the guys came around the back of the truck, stated (Sarge) start your search here. There was this huge row of buildings on both sides of a very long block that had barbed wire and a huge sign with print, *'PHYSICIANS ON SITE/CONDOMS SUPPLIED/KEEP YOURSELF SAFE. PRACTICE SAFETY FIRST, THE WORLD IS YOUR OYSTER'*. This place was a red light area. Wall to wall whorehouses, government inspected for the fleet that docked in the bay just outside of the entire area of this coast.

This block, this area was, the midway of Viet Nam. The supply subway for the North and Middle Viet Nam. This Da Lat was like the Saigon of the South. One big Quarter Master Supply Headquarters for the multiple Armed Forces. Not far from Da Nang, Pleiku, the open seaport, the airport performed for all of the Armed Forces, the complete NATO forces were up here, French, Austrian, African, Brits, American Roc, Swedes, Turks, everybody. This area was a Mecca of activity. What had we stumbled into?

Now, all I had as a contact was Spec 5 Anderson's communication and his company I.D. He would be on the look out for us, and a big "no sweat". It was the Company that was housed in a big hotel building in the heart of this place. It had a desk clerk, elevators, huge dining room, pool, tennis courts, sauna, gardens and the (bad part) some cats that were real white boys. Good ole nigger hating white boys from down South USA. I was almost "alley, alley, in free" when the other shoe dropped like a ton of bricks. We had a huge suite, the quarters were divided into bays, two large shower rooms and toilets, large open space in the middle to lounge around in, beautifully furnished. Nice, real nice. All was well until about 2:00 a.m. or 3:00 a.m. that second night when the MA came. Reports of the

GIs from down South and the possible deserters from the 101st from up North hiding out, looking for his whore. Now, just hearing this pissed me off aside from being caught, told on and having my brother men involved and now locked up with me, miles away from where they were suppose to be. Plus, poor E-5 Anderson didn't even really know any of us (on a real tip). This whole event was real fed up!

Now, Sergeant Hernandez had pull with the 716th, 504th, 503rd and several other Military Police Groups, because he had been in the Marines, Air Force and now Army in his 20 some odd years of service, but I had not heard him talk of the Navy. I knew we were doomed to be hung, or locked away forever. My heart fell, once again handcuffed, riding in the back of a Jeep but a covered hard top Jeep. This time to a brick building, but still a jail off we went.

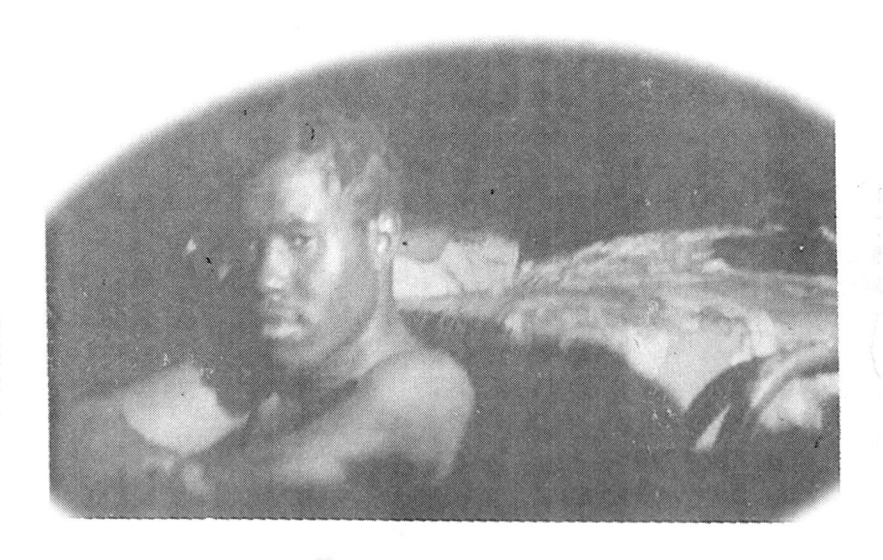

After a jive booking, a long sit down in cells, then called upon one at a time to this room. I guess I was last, a long table, two Officers, a young court typist taking shorthand and a young guy as my advisor, not lawyer but advisor. As he introduced himself, because I was guilty as sin, I sat there quiet as a mouse for minutes, then "Sergeant Walker, SSN, Service Number, 101st Airborne Desk Log Ammo, USV Long Bien Post, Southeast Asia/426, 533 Batt HQ & HQ Company, Camp Eagle A Company, a Philly Pad 101st Airborne, Phu Bia Company, Attachment 1/501 Infantry Phu Bia Viet Nam, correct son?" "Naw!" Wait MACV HQ and HQ Company, A Company, Saigon City, Saigon South Viet Nam." "Is that correct son?" 'What the hell are you doing in our Operational Theater?" And I began to answer and I must have talked for two hours or so.

When I stopped, we broke for lunch, fed up. The panel looked drained when we had broke for lunch, almost baffled if my story was but one big lie or something. Well, two days later with all of the confirmation they had compiled, they called all of us before them. We must have stood at attention for at least 10-15 minutes, just standing there, them staring at us. Then the Major (Army guy) spoke. "You men have broke every rule possible to Military Code of Conduct, possible desertion, AWOL, theft, piracy, hijacking, forgery, impersonation, trespassing, commandeering vehicles, involving others in your shame and numerous other violations during a time of war. You should all be shot, hung from a yard arm, burnt at a stake. But it's now up to us to decide this. Your own supervisors will dish out Military justice upon you!" "Do you understand?" We replied, "Yes Sir". Then to our surprise, the major laughed and said "Only GIs could pull a crop of shit off like this. This is real, fucking real, holy shit, fucking cool!"

After being dismissed, I awaited sentencing before the panel. I was given bunkler line maintenance for the remainder of my tour along with Company area clean up man (shit head's job) I cleaned shit houses (dump pans) started the shower heaters for the Company showers, cleaned the formation parade field, not to mention worked the perimeter line for the Post for booby traps left overnight by Charlie. Plus this Company job let everybody know I was in the shit again. One thing this status gave me was a window to clean up. To stay clean from drugs sometimes is a good thing. I came to learn during my time on lock in. It helped more than it hurt. Being close to phones, I could speak to Headquarters down South very easily and I did over and over. I kept up on what was going on. I was working on trying to get information on how to get my son, citizenship for the USA and if possible papers also for Hue". To tell the truth, I had been told it would be hard to get papers for Hue' but a Visa might be in order because I would have to remarry Hue' on American soil for the marriage to be accepted by the USA and the U.S. Army, especially for benefits. But the kid was ok, he was mine and he was born in the USA Army Hospital on Post which was USA properties or USA territory, so he was half American (Negro) (a home boy). Mein Dan, bonifide.

    Now, how to pull it together to get him or them back to America? I had Bro. Rochester checking into things, also Hue' was checking things out. She was all worked up about going to the USA. Bro. Portsmouth and the entire staff at Long Bien Post was checking into the matter for me. But, I had not taken into consideration the stress, not on me but on mother and child unborn. Now, I had gathered the woman and child, got them transportation to Saigon, had my court martial, got away with minimal damage again, no jail time, only losing one stripe, plus pay. I still had plenty of contacts, but I forgot about that creep.

Chapter 14
My Son is Born

The Major, the snake was still in there pitching, plus Hue', low down *Ma Ma* San. Hue' went into unexpected labor and almost died I was told. The kid had turned like a top. I heard the cord was wrapped all around his throat, choking him out. The kid was almost gray colored at birth. The hero, the Major, rushed Hue' and my newborn son up to the Veteran Medical Hospital in his Jeep to save both of them for Hue' had started bleeding from between her legs and the midwife couldn't stop the bleeding. The Major had also signed Hue' in the hospital as his woman with child or she wouldn't have gotten treatment as a nationalist of Viet Nam and the infant was registered as his son. I kicked the desk over in the orderly room as I heard this. My First Sergeant thought I had lost my mind again and had me restrained to a chair held by three GIs. When I settled down, I told First Sergeant what had come off. All he did was shook his head and slowly walked away. Later that evening as I was leaving the orderly room, I stopped out the door to be met by two MPs. First Sergeant walked up, told me I was under house arrest. "Why"? I asked. "To keep you from getting in real trouble son. I know you are thinking of running back to Saigon, aren't you son?" I didn't open my mouth. I just stood there. Up to my hootch I started, but I was steered towards the supply room. Once there, the door was reinforced with a big steel bar, wire screen and a lock hasp mounted on the door. I was really being put under arrest. They fed me, poured water on me for showers, exercised me all within eye shot of that supply room, no work, no formations, no movies no visits from anyone. Just First Sergeant, and he didn't say much. All I could do was think and think of ways to kill the Major and Hue's dog mother. Yea, to kill the both of them. Just to get to that phone in the orderly room would be all I needed, just a two minute phone call to down South. Just one call! I tried hollering across to fellow GIs but orders were to leave Walker alone, stay clear. And every damn man sure did.

Then, either lost in time or I lost my mind, two months had passed and I was told by First Sergeant I was getting short (short) what? Panic! Panic set in, short, I had less than 40 days left in the country! They were not going to offer me another tour either for any reason (I had too many infractions) too many Articles 15 too many court martials. They wanted me out of the country! First Sergeant said I was fucked! I begged to use the phone. No, I was told. Was I going to be considered to be released from this supply room, no I was told never, never, except to get on a plane and be shipped to the States, First Sergeant said. This blew my mind and I performed. I ransacked the supply room. They called the MPs, handcuffed me to the flagpole. I sat there in the heat, in the dark, and it began to rain. I was covered by a poncho by First Sergeant. He sat in the orderly room watching me all night long. I dug First Sergeant, he looked after me, he talked to me like a father, gave me a lot of breaks but if I had gotten loose during that time, who knows what would have happened. Then, First Sergeant had the supply room straightened up, released me back to my cage, no more hooked up to the flagpole, but I still wanted to kill everybody that came near.

Time had passed, it was time now to get ready to leave the country. A program called Project Transition from the war was being implemented. All it was, was a jailhouse arrest for GIs with MPs to guard you. Big wire fences, barbed wired fences 14 feet tall, buildings with guarded tower all about to watch inside and outside the perimeter to keep the dope dealers away and to dry the junkie GIs out before leaving Viet Nam. All GIs stayed there for 14 days processing out and drying out at the same time, piss test every other day for drugs. The days were long and being flown down to Da Nang only to be caged in holding camps didn't sit well with any of us GIs. Yes, these holding camps were only four miles from the Da Nang Airport.

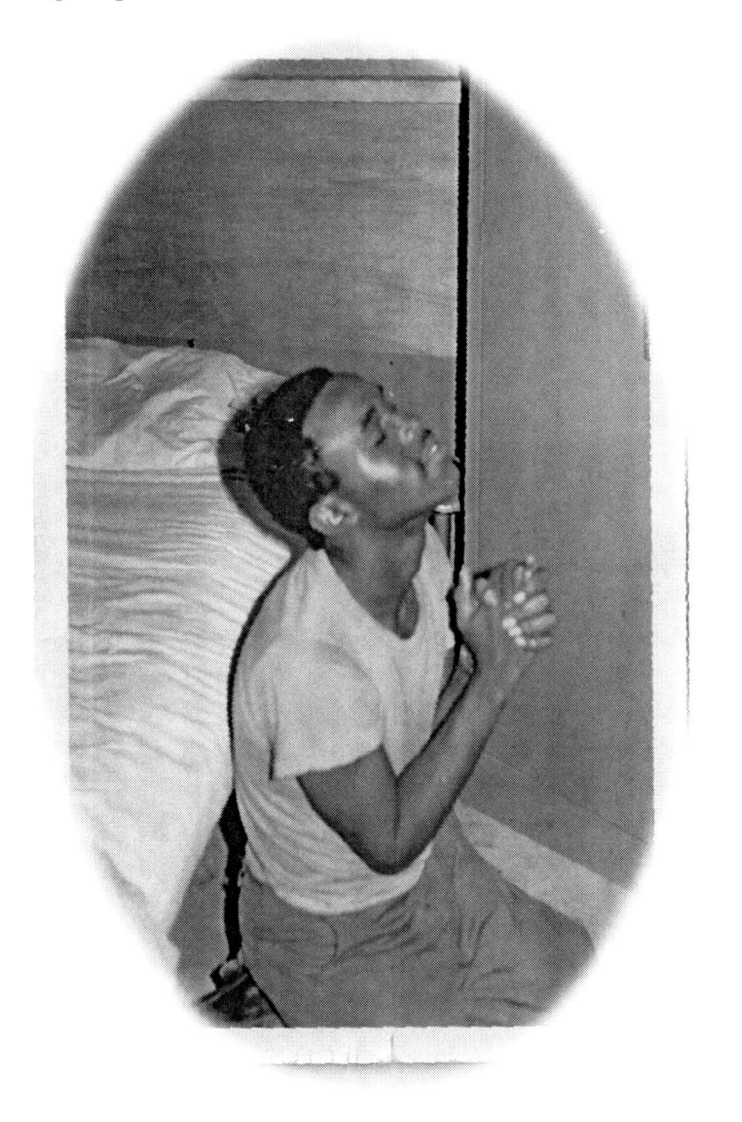

212 | A MEIN DAN VIETNAM

Chapter 15
Leaving Viet Nam

So, out of the camps, straight onto the planes and on towards to Ft. Lewis, Washington, Washington State, USA, home of the brave. The phone was accessible to every GI in the camp. But there were about 1,000 GIs in lines that seem to never end. I gave up trying to wait my turn. I mostly sat around. I was all but beaten down. I had blown everything. No word with Saigon in months, no contact with Bro. Rochester. Bro. Gator Man had left the country by now. My only hope was that Hue' and the kid were souvenirs of the Major. Hue's mother was dead of dry rot and ate up by rats. But I still had a plan when I got back to Ft. Lewis, Washington. I do my last 6 months there and be a good GI, earn my stripes back, wait for my re-up offer, then return to Viet Nam and take my girl and child back after I killed the Major in cold blood! That is the plan! Yea, this I can do, come on with it. Come on iron bird, take me home. I'll be back here again real soon for I am MEIN DAN.

This is to be but a temporary halt, 1, 2; the march is on. My child, my girl and home was left there so "damn" bet you, I will be back, this is not over with.

The story continues…

A MEIN DAN VIETNAM

To Blondie
Thank you for your support!!

Peace &
Blessings
Sybil B Walker
(wife)